AMERICA BETRAYED

ONE STEP FROM COLLAPSE

by
Dewey Goldsmith

AuthorHouse™
1663 Liberty Drive, Suite 200
Bloomington, IN 47403
www.authorhouse.com
Phone: 1-800-839-8640

First published by AuthorHouse   6/30/2008

ISBN: 978-1-4343-8797-4 (sc)
ISBN: 978-1-4343-8796-7 (hc)

Printed in the United States of America
Bloomington, Indiana

This book is printed on acid-free paper.

Table of Contents

INTRODUCTION. 3

CONSTITUTIONAL AMENDMENT XVI 11

CREATING A WELFARE STATE. 21

JOINING THE UNITED NATIONS 29

CREATING A CONTROLLED MEDIA 43

DESTROYING OUR INDUSTRIAL BASE. 49

ABOLISHING OUR CONSTITUTION. 67

DESTROY THE CHRISTIAN BASE 77

DISARMING AMERICA 85

DISARMING AMERICA 93

THE COLLAPSE OF AMERICA. 111

AUTHORS VIEWPOINT 133

INTRODUCTION

I believe it is safe to say that many of our citizens have never really studied the history of how America came into being. For the benefit of all here is a brief recap of history. England was a country ruled by an unelected royal monarchy. Laws were made by the king and enforced by the king's loyal enforcers. Citizens had no rights and were heavily taxed by the king. Dissenters were killed or imprisoned. As the means to travel by sea became available stouthearted people left England and came to a new land now known as America.

But the king's men followed and for a time enforced the king's laws and taxes upon the people in this new land. But the flame of liberty burned brightly in the hearts of our fathers, as reflected in the words of Patrick Henry, "I know not what course others may follow, but as for myself, give me liberty or give me death". Thus a rebellion was formed and the people declared their independence from the tyranny of the King of England.

One can't help but question whether our leaders in Washington have ever read the declaration of independence issued by our forefathers on the 4th day of July in the year 1776.

For their benefit excerpts from that declaration of independence is herein provided: It reads; we hold these truths to be self evident, that all men are created equal, that they are endowed by their creator with certain unalienable rights, that among these rights are life, liberty and the pursuit of happiness. That to secure these rights, Governments are instituted among men, deriving their powers from the consent of the governed, That whenever any form of government becomes destructive of these ends, it is the right of the people to alter or abolish it, and to institute new government, laying it's foundation on such principles and organizing it's powers in such form, as to them shall seem most likely to effect their safety and happiness.

After a long struggle the people won their independence and a new nation came into being, a nation consisting of thirteen colonies. The colonies established a flimsy national government governed by the Articles of Confederation. But our forefathers did not stop there. Being free without a foundation to secure that freedom would insure that freedom would not last.

They devoted their lives to establishing a government that would govern by the consent of the people. A government based upon foundations and principles, and organized in such manner most likely to affect their safety and happiness. Our forefathers then devoted their lives to insuring that the principles of Divine creation, would be established and preserved for the people, preserved in the form of a Constitution, which included the Bill of Rights preserving the rights, liberties and justice for the people.

One must question whether our governmental leaders have read or studied the ten amendments, called the Bill of Rights, which the founders of our constitutional form of government included in our constitution. For their benefit, and the benefit of all, I have included the Bill of Rights Amendments herein in the hope they will read and study it, then return government to the people, and govern by the consent of the people.

Amendment No. 1 states: Congress shall make no law respecting an establishment of religion, or prohibiting the free exercise thereof; or abridging the freedom of speech, or of the press, or of the right of the people to assemble, and to petition the government for a redress of grievances. (In view of the passage of the McCain Feingold law prohibiting the peoples voicing their opinion sixty days prior to an election, it appears our congress, the president and the court believe they have the power to dissolve our rights to free speech and freedom of the press.)

Amendment No. 2 states: A well regulated militia, being necessary to the security of a free state, the right of the people to keep and bear arms, shall not be infringed. (More about this later)

Amendment No. 3 states: No soldier shall, in time of peace, be quartered in any house without the consent of the owner, neither in time of war, but in a manner prescribed by law.

Amendment No. 4 states: The right of the people to be secure in their persons, houses, papers and effects, against unreasonable searches and seizures, shall not be violated, and no warrant shall issue, but upon probable cause, supported by oath or affirmation, and particularly describing the place to be searched, and the person or things to be searched.

(Would you agree our leaders seem to discount the importance of this amendment, in view of the fact they approve random roadblocks where they stop, detain and search citizens for proof of insurance, licenses and use of alcohol. And this is done without probable cause or warrant. Where does the constitution give government the right to violate the rights of all, in the hope of finding one who might have violated some law?)

Amendment No. 5 States: No person shall be held to answer for a capital, or otherwise infamous crime, unless on a presentment or indictment of a grand jury, except in cases arising in the land or naval forces, or in the militia, when in actual service in time of war or public danger; nor shall any person be subject for the same offense to be twice put in jeopardy of life or limb; nor shall be compelled in any criminal case to be a witness against himself, nor be deprived of life, liberty or property, without due process of law, nor shall private property be taken for public use, without just compensation.

Amendment No. 6 states: In all criminal prosecutions, the accused shall enjoy the right to a speedy trial, by an impartial jury of the state and district wherein the crime shall have been committed, which district shall have been previously ascertained by law, and to be informed of the nature and cause of the accusation; to be confronted with the witnesses against him, to have compulsory process for obtaining witnesses in his favor, and to have the assistance of Counsel for his defense.

Amendment No. 7 states: In suits at common law, where the value in controversy shall exceed twenty dollars, the right to trial by jury shall be preserved, and no fact tried by jury, shall be otherwise reexamined in any court of the United States, than according to the rules of common law.

Amendment No. 8 states: Excessive bail shall not be required, nor excessive fines imposed, nor cruel and unusual punishments inflicted.

Amendment No. 9 states: The enumeration in the Constitution, of certain rights, shall not be construed to deny or disparage others retained by the people. (In plain simple words this amendment says; the rights of the people are not limited to only those rights stated in the constitution, and government cannot deny or disparage other rights by claiming they are not stated in the constitution. This Amendment has been totally ignored and abused by government and the courts.)

Amendment No. 10 states: The powers not delegated to the United States by the Constitution, nor prohibited by it to the states, are reserved to the States respectively, or to the people. Like amendment no. 9; this Amendment restricts the powers of government to only those powers enumerated, stated, in the Constitution. It reserves all other powers to the states, or to the people. A right does not have to be stated in the constitution for the people to claim that right; The Constitution limits the power of government, it does not limit the rights of the people; Our founders wrote it that way to protect the people from an oppressive government like we now have.

I believe it is also safe to say few citizens have ever seriously studied our constitution or Bill of Rights. How they came to be written. How they changed the lives of citizens then and are still changing our lives today. Our forefathers, the founders of our country, were well aware of the dangers of existing under an all powerful central government. They devoted their lives and fortunes to insure the people of this new land would never have to submit to tyrannical rule. They then formed a constitution and Bill of Rights to insure it would never happen in America.

After several years of devoted effort a national constitution was completed. By June of 1778 eight of the required nine states had ratified that constitution. But the state of Virginia, led by Patrick Henry and George Mason, refused to ratify that constitution because it did not provide for or protect the rights of the people. In order to get the State of Virginia to ratify it the other eight states had to guarantee the delegates from Virginia that a bill of rights identifying and protecting the rights of individual citizens would be included. With that guarantee Virginia ratified the constitution and it became our Constitution on March 4th, 1789.

That constitution spells out the powers and authorities of the federal government, The Congress, the executive and judicial branches, and to a lesser extent the powers of the states. Patrick Henry and George Mason stood firm in their arguments for citizen's rights and finally, two years later, ten constitutional amendments were adopted in the year 1791. These amendments became known as the citizens Bill of Rights. Many have said the constitution was the greatest document ever written, and to be sure it is the best ever to be written.

However, the importance of the Bill of Rights and the rights, liberties and protections it grants citizens far outweighs the importance of the constitution by itself. All ten amendments delegate and protect the individual's rights to live ones life free of government oppression. The constitution delegates certain powers to the central and state governments. It limit's the powers of government specifically to only those powers delegated to it. The Bill of Rights grants all powers, not delegated to government, to the people. That's all rights, not just those specifically identified and stated in the constitution.

I am forced to question whether our Presidents, members of Congress and our Judicial appointees have studied these documents. I must question whether they have not, or whether they choose to ignore them. Consider this one example of how the constitution and Bill of Rights has been rationalized and ignored in the halls of congress. We hear a lot of discussion regarding the second amendment, "A well regulated militia, being necessary to the security of a free state, the right of the people to keep and bear arms shall not be infringed".

The Socialists and Federal control advocates in congress and those who seek a Moslem led new world order fear this amendment above all others. They argue this amendment gives only those serving in military uniform the right to bear firearms. If we give in to that doctrine we will soon be like those who were disarmed by Hitler, Stalin and all other Dictators who enslaved an unarmed people. We will be in the same condition England, Australia and Canada is in today. Overrun by violent crime and without the means to defend ourselves from criminals or an oppressive socialist government.

To argue that the second amendment refers to a states right to form a militia infers: that the founders were so ignorant they contradicted themselves by stating in article one of the constitution, congress has the authority to limit the right of the states to form militia to wartime periods only, then stated in the second amendment that the power of the state to form militias shall not be infringed.

There is no contradiction. The profound clarity and purposeful wording of the constitution and bill of rights belies the interpretation made by the Washington socialists.

The constitution identifies specific powers delegated the government, while the bill of rights preserves all other rights for the people. The right of the people to keep and bear arms does not have to be enumerated, stated, in the Constitution for the people to have that right; for all rights belong to the people unless given to the government in the constitution. And the constitution does not delegate government the right to decide who shall keep and bear firearms.

In the second amendment the founders are protecting the people's right to keep and bear arms, not the states power to form militias. For the peoples right to keep and bear firearms is also addressed in two other Bill of Rights Amendments; the Ninth (IX) and Tenth (10) Amendments. The importance of these two amendments, the ninth and tenth amendments, are far too often overlooked by the people, and ignored by government and the courts. The federal government has only those rights enumerated in the constitution; all other rights belong to the people. And the constitution does not delegate to the federal government the authority to decide who shall enjoy the right of being armed and capable of defending our country.

The constitution and bill of rights changed the lives of all citizens then and for all who followed. The people found they could pursue life, liberty and happiness in their own way free of government intrusions and infringements. This worked well for two centuries and our nation and the people thrived. Today our executive, congressional and judicial branches of government consistently adopt laws and issue opinions depriving citizens of their rights using the argument that those rights are not enumerated in the constitution or bill of rights.

But even more dangerous to a free people the Washington Socialists do so using the argument the constitution is not a permanent document for all times. That it is a living document that must be interpreted differently to meet changing times.

The founders of our republic and framers of our constitution said one and all; they have given us a free nation but warned that it would last only as long as the people had the courage to protect and preserve the constitution.

In this book I have identified the ominous growth of federal government, how that growth occurred and where it is taking America. Fear of government is now a more controlling emotion than love of country. Courage has been replaced by apathy as the most prominent trait of the people. We have become as sheep blindly following our leaders down the path to national collapse.

Imagine your children facing life under these conditions. America was no longer a sovereign nation. There is no national constitution. There is no Citizens Bill of Rights. Your children now exist under the rule of the New World Order, controlled by anti American and anti Christian Moslem and Socialist leaders. There is no Social Security, Veterans pensions, civil service pensions, 401K pensions or state teacher's pensions.

What if the medical care provided by our government operated socialized hospitals and state controlled medical practitioners resembled the care one gets in the Moslem led states of Asia, Europe, Africa, South America and the Middle East. The pestilence and diseases such as Aids, Plague, Small Pox and Tuberculosis carried in by the hordes of immigrants has spread across what was once America. The elder citizens have long departed, the grandfathers and grandmothers are no more, and the fathers and mothers are dying of starvation and disease before their children's eyes.

How will your children feel when they wake up some day to find America had collapsed? How will your children feel when they are alone, enslaved and starving for love and food? Or will your children never know the love of life and peace because our apathy and malaise allowed the socialists in Washington to destroy our national sovereignty. What chance will they have when the hordes of Moslems from United Nations states come in and take over our land.

In this book I have identified and discussed the steps that lead to national collapse, where I believe America is today, and what the future holds. I must caution you; like the steps to the hanging gallows the steps to national collapse are limited, and America is fast approaching that last step.

Constitutional Amendment XVI

The predictable and approaching collapse of America can be traced to its beginning, the adoption of the sixteenth amendment to our constitution. Our founders warned us of many things, among which, was their belief that if the federal government ever gained the power to tax the people a free America would not last. In 1913 America took the first step towards national collapse when they gave Washington the authority to tax the people's earnings. Since then our leaders in Washington have never looked back. They have kept their eyes on our earnings and their hands in our pockets and the spending has never stopped.

In 1913 our constitution was amended granting the federal government the power to lay and collect taxes on the peoples incomes, from whatever source derived, without apportionment among the several states, and without regard to any census or enumeration. Granting the congress the power to tax the peoples earnings was the gravest mistake ever made by the states. With the power to tax now in the hands of congress, it was only a question of time until they would use that power to expand the reach of the federal government until they controlled every aspect of the peoples lives.

Seizures of property and intrusions of personal privacy were common in old England, and they are becoming so in America today. Many families have seen the homes they worked and saved to purchase, the homes they have lived in and raised their families in, seized by our government under the public domain laws. Seized by government officials and given to wealthy contributors, to use for their own private investment purposes, in ways that would generate more revenue for government. This is only one example of how life under our government today is becoming like it was under the King of England. There are many other similarities, but it was the Kings abuse of power by so called taxing (stealing the workers properties and incomes) that drove the people to leave England, and declare their independence in the land we call America.

Before the adoption of the sixteenth amendment in 1913, the constitution granted the federal government specific, and limited, power to lay and collect taxes, duties, imports and excises uniformly (from the states, not the people). The states provided the federal government funds to pay the cost of Defense, Commerce and promote the General Welfare of the United States, and pay the cost of operating the government. But the federal government did not have the constitutional authority to tax the people's earnings.

The founders of our country also warned us not to enter into treaties with foreign countries, because to do so would lead to wars and uncontrolled spending. But with the peoples earnings now within reach of corrupt government leaders in Washington spending was no longer a problem, they could always take more from the working peoples earnings. So our leaders ignored the advice of our forefathers and started an era of treaties, wars and spending. The result has been fifty years of wars, conflicts, and foreign aid spending.

Once Washington had the power to tax our earnings it began trying to buy the loyalty of foreign leaders with so called foreign aid programs. Trillions of dollars of our earnings have been taken in taxes and given to foreign despots under the guise of aid. Whether it was called lend lease or foreign aid the results were the same. Washington has been taking your earnings and giving it to foreign rulers and the New World Order Socialist leaders for six decades. It has forced millions of working families into bankruptcy and foreclosures, left the federal government insolvent, ten trillion dollars in debt and destroyed the value of American currency.

During the period between 1779, when our constitution was adopted, until 1913 when the sixteenth amendment was adopted, the people and our nation prospered. People could work and use their earnings to build a better life for themselves, their families and their communities. The people and the country thrived and became the envy of the world. They started small family businesses and used their earnings to build a future for their families and communities. Many others worked, invested their earnings, and saw their small businesses grow into successful enterprises.

They used their earnings to develop a system of community schools where their children could learn and prosper. In these schools children learned the three R's, but even more important, they learned the value of a principled life, based upon Christian values, which is no longer permitted in our dumb them down public schools. The accomplishments they made were many and changed the world for all times to come. America became the most highly educated and advanced nation in the world. Advancements in medicine, agricultural technologies and industry raised the living standards for all American families. And the people prospered and saved for their children's futures.

Electricity was invented that gave us the ability to see at night, heat our homes, cool our homes and operate our tools and equipment. The tools and equipment used in industry and in our every day lives came from their earnings and the educational opportunities it provided. Not from a public school system where government controlled and established a curriculum without guiding principles. The people's untaxed earnings brought us the telephones, radios, televisions, computers, airplanes, automobiles, steam locomotives and hundreds of other inventions. Products that would not have come had not the people had their earnings to educate themselves and family. Just as important, the people had their untaxed earnings and the freedom to use their earnings and their imagination to better themselves and their communities.

With federal revenues restricted to revenues derived from the states, the central government, now known as the federal government, had to conserve and apply revenues to meet specific necessary responsibilities. Maintaining a national defense as necessary, identifying and regulating commerce between the states and keeping the central government in operation. Thus, the Constitution limited the role of federal government. The founders of our country and our Constitution and Bill of Rights intentionally limited the Federal governments power to tax in order to prevent any accumulation of power sufficient to overrun the states authority and the people's rights.

As originally established positions in the congress were temporary. That is, the congress was to meet annually, conduct necessary business, then adjourn. It was established as a part time position. Legislators were paid out of the treasury, an amount specified by law, from revenues furnished by the states. This procedure limited the amount legislators could waste or give themselves for their services. You want to know why you have no earnings left. Turn your television to C-span and watch the legislators give themselves and their supporting contributor's new perks, now called earmarks, and buy votes with your taxes.

In the early congresses most legislators had family businesses and employment at home. Serving as a legislator then was truly a service, not a lifetime profession called service. As a result they spent only the time at the capital necessary to keep the central government in operation. This meant most of the time they were at home away from their legislative positions. They were not sitting in the back rooms of their legislative offices making deals and spending the people's earnings.

But passage of the sixteenth amendment changed all that. With all the peoples earnings now within the reach of government, and no controls on how it was used, the spending commenced in earnest. Agencies and departments were created for no other purpose than to expand the power and reach of government. Naturally they had to create the Internal Revenue Department to determine what earnings to tax and how much income to take from the people. Then they had to extend that bureaucracy to collect the taxes they decided to seize. And of course they had to establish a federal enforcement agency to insure the peoples compliance. And naturally, the more that bureaucracy grew the more government managers and taxes it took to keep it operating.

Then the Social security system was started, for a worthwhile cause initially, to provide elder citizens some measure of personal control and life's necessities. That required the formation of a social security Department, and the necessary employees to run the system.

Unfortunately the Congress expanded the program time and time again, until it became something it was not intended for, a retirement program for all citizens. And again, the larger the system became the more people and taxes it took to keep it going.

Then the congress saw all that tax money in the social security fund and decided they wanted it. So they changed the law and gave themselves the power to steal the people's social security trust funds and waste it on their pet projects from which they could secure votes and political support. And they got away with it because they make the law to suit their own purpose. Then after they spent the social security trust funds they had to take more taxes from the people to keep the system going. And the cost to keep the system going keeps growing, and the taxes the people have to pay to meet that cost is still increasing year by year.

If you were the manager of another persons investment account, and you took that fund and used it for other purposes to benefit yourself, you would be appropriately charged and tried for theft. The social security trust fund was the peoples investment fund built by the deposits collected from the peoples earnings.

Does the fact that a group of people, our elected congressional representatives, got together and decided to take our investment funds make it right. I don't believe it does. Because of their misuse of our investment funds we are paying higher taxes, and there will be no investment returns for our children.

During the period since the congress was given the power to tax the people's earnings, the size of government has doubled time and time again. As new agencies and Departments were created, a purpose for those agencies and departments had to be developed. Then offices had to be constructed to house them. And of course thousands of new employees had to be recruited to fill the offices. Lets see, there was the Housing and Urban Development (HUD) department, the Department of Transportation, the Department of Education, the Federal Labor Department, Medicare department, The National Defense Department, the federal Bureau of Investigation, the Central Intelligence Agency, The Bureau of Alcohol and Firearms, and finally the Homeland Security Department. Just to name a few.

With each new department came the need for higher taxes to defray their cost and most important came the opportunity for nepotistic hiring to reward friends, relatives and political contributors with high paying managerial positions in those newly created departments. Then as government grew and the number of employees grew, a Civil Service Department had to be created to oversee the pay and entitlements of the employees and administrators. If the private sector ran their businesses like the congress does there would not be one successful thriving business in the country.

But more important of all to the legislators, with each new department came the opportunity to expand the reach of the federal government into the lives of private citizens. The federal government became the largest employer in the country. Then they established the federal employees retirement program. The object was to make as many citizens as possible dependent upon the federal government for their livelihood. Those who depend upon government for their monthly income can be controlled.

It didn't take the greedy power hungry federal legislators long to find a way to reward themselves. First they established the need to make their positions as legislators full time positions with no limit on the number of years they could occupy their offices. And with the ever increasing size of government that wasn't hard to do. And they could then claim an annual salary as full time legislators, with all the perks that come with it, instead of part time legislators.

Next they decided they could and did establish their own salaries and benefits. They could meet during the night time hours to vote themselves increases, establish generous non contributory pensions for themselves and free medical care for themselves and their families. In short, they created such a lavish lifestyle for themselves they spent more time raising money to stay in power than they did minding the store. And for years, before the law was finally changed, they could raise tens of millions in reelection contributions and keep for themselves what they didn't use to stay in power.

Then they decided the best way to insure reelection was to create programs that gave large sums of money to certain classes of society, thereby insuring their vote in future elections. Whether they were called the great society, the fair deal, the new deal, or just plain welfare the results were the same. It relieved these classes of the responsibility of going to school, securing a job and providing for themselves.

Tens of millions of people no longer had to consider finding and keeping employment. After all the government would provide them a place to live, buy their food, pay their utilities, their medical expenses and give them spending money as well. So why work or worry about caring for the next child. After all, the more children they have the more taxpayers assistance they would receive. And the cost in increased taxes on those who worked grew and grew.

These vote getting programs not only resulted in, they encouraged the increasing numbers of people dependent upon government for their every need. These programs increased the number of children born of single mothers out of wedlock. These programs resulted in tens of millions of citizens, of every age, having the time to stand on the street corners committing prostitution, using drugs and committing crimes of every kind and description.

These programs resulted in forty million unemployed or under employed citizens becoming totally dependent upon government for their every need. You can correct me if I'm wrong but I believe most programs mentioned above were sponsored and adopted by the Democratic Congress, with the help of some republicans. These programs garnered enough votes to insure we had a socialist democratic congress for nearly all of the past sixty years.

But these are not the only vote getting giveaway programs the congress has adopted. There were plenty of gifts to the middle class and wealthy as well.

There was the farm subsidies, peanut subsidies, tobacco subsidies, the oil subsidies, the defense industry subsidies, corporate tax subsidies and many other programs aimed at securing the votes and support of these classes of citizens.

Programs that permitted American corporations to move an industry or office offshore thus evading corporate taxes. Again you can correct me if I'm wrong but I believe these programs were sponsored by the republican party, with the help of some democratic congressional members. But while these programs brought in a lot of political money for individual republican politicians, they did not bring in large class votes in numbers sufficient to give the republican party control of the congress for long periods of time.

Whether these vote seeking giveaway programs were sponsored by the Democratic or Republican parties the end results were the same. It takes money to fund federal programs and the sixteenth amendment gave congress the power to raise that money by imposing and increasing taxes on those who work for a living. What started out as income tax to fund necessary federal defense and commerce needs and to defray the cost of running the federal government turned into a working families nightmare. To make up for the loss of income grabbed by the legislators, working men had to work at two jobs and their wives had to work, leaving the children at home alone.

One result of giving congress the right to tax our earnings was to see the states, counties and municipalities follow suit. Before long there was state income taxes, state property taxes, state highway taxes, state sales taxes and others too numerous to mention. Then came the city income taxes, city school taxes, county mental health taxes, county senior citizen taxes and anything else they can dream up a need for. One tax that really drove people mad was city income taxes collected from any person who worked inside a city limits. Even if they didn't reside in the city, and couldn't vote on city issues or political candidates, they still have to pay the tax. Wasn't taxation without representation the primary reason for the revolution from England.

Now our corrupt officials do the same thing and our courts allow them to do so. What does that say about the direction our government is taking the country?

Today when we add up the federal income tax, social security tax, Medicare tax, Gasoline tax, highway tax, and sales taxes; then add in state income tax, state property taxes, state sales taxes, state Medicare taxes and all other state taxes, then add in the county taxes and municipal taxes the average working person only gets to keep about forty cents of every dollar earned. Yesterday the younger generation worked and took care of their parents and grandparents. Today our young people don't have enough left from their earnings to care for themselves, so the elder citizens are now dependent upon government for their needs. Without question, giving congress the power to tax the people's earnings was the most destructive thing the people could have done to themselves and our country.

Our forefathers had vision and the courage and faith to pursue their vision. More important they had their earnings they could use to better themselves, their families, and build a strong nation. They pursued their vision and America became a nation of free people, the most resourceful people the world has ever seen.

They moved west, north and south across the land building towns and cities as they went. They developed manufacturing, industrial and agricultural enterprises such as the world had never seen. They saved and invested their untaxed earnings to make America a better place for themselves and their families.

But with the adoption of the sixteenth Amendment the people were taxed into indebtedness and their resourcefulness has been replaced by apathy and malaise. Elected officials became spenders of the peoples earnings instead of servants who govern by the consent of the people. The peoples courage was replaced by fear of government, and our nation was started on the road to decay and collapse. The sixteenth Amendment was the first step, the deciding step, that started our nation on the road to collapse.

CREATING A WELFARE STATE

Welfare: The second most damaging step taken by Washington that will eventually lead to national collapse was the policy that started America on the road to Socialism. The Great Society was a set of domestic programs proposed or enacted upon the initiative of President Lyndon B. Johnson. New major Federal spending programs were launched during the period of the implementation of the Great Society. It resembled the New Deal domestic agenda of Franklin Roosevelt however greatly expanded. It included Medicare, Medicaid, Federal Education funding, Urban Assistance and other programs which turned into all forms of welfare, subsidized housing, food stamps and free medical care.

The implementation of welfare to assist those who could not help themselves soon turned into a program to help those who didn't want to work and help themselves. It became a bonanza for those who choose not to conduct themselves in an acceptable manner capable of caring for themselves. People who choose to breed or be bred out of wedlock found government would compensate them for their behaviors, at the taxpayers expense. The more children they had the more welfare they would receive. We now have, according to whose estimates you read, as many as seventy percent of newborn babies born to some classes, born out of wedlock.

Again, according to whose numbers you use, we now have as many as fifty million citizens collecting some form of welfare subsidies. What started out as a free handout of food stamps once a month has turned into a taxpayers handout for those who don't want to work and brings in class votes for the politicians who keep the programs expanding. Welfare now provides free medical care and medication, free housing or lodging at subsidized rates in taxpayers built housing developments. It now includes free food, utilities and automobiles. Yes that's right, free automobiles. No wonder the numbers of those taking advantage of welfare has increased by millions since the program was started.

And what about the cost of nepotistic hiring to fill the need for employees and managers of these programs. Adding the cost of providing a welfare, oops, social services office, in each of the counties in every state, plus the multiple offices located in large municipalities we easily have a total of 5,000 such offices. These require a total staff on payroll running into the tens of millions. The total cost just to staff and maintain these offices adds hundreds of billions to the federal budget and millions to our state budgets as well. And that doesn't count the hundreds of billions of dollars it cost to furnish all the freebies to those with their hands out.

If we add in the cost of building and staffing hundreds of federal and state prisons to furnish free food, telephone service, cable television, medical attention, recreational centers and lodging for the welfare recipients turned criminals we see hundreds of billions added to federal and state budgets. We must not forget the thousands of additional federal, state, county and municipal law enforcement officers required to maintain order in our city streets nor the billions that adds to the cost of federal, state and local law enforcement agencies. These high rising costs are a direct result of welfare programs that compensate people who would rather hang out on the street corners, committing crimes and using drugs than go to school or work.

There is another class of citizens who love government handouts. Take a look at those so called senior citizens. They sit and gripe about the free handouts given to those who don't want to work then hold their hands out for their own benefits. Lets see, we have the meals on wheels, senior citizens taxi service, senior citizens centers and reduced property taxes under the homestead act and loads of other options. Someone has to pay for all these senior citizens services, guess who. We do, those of us who are working for a living with the governments tax collectors hand in our pockets. For the working it's pay, pay, pay without end.

And what about the Washington politicians. Who's paying for their lavish life style? Their inflated salaries, free obscene non-contributory retirement plans. Who's paying for their free medical, dental and eyeglass coverage.

Who pays for their vacation junkets around the world and across America. We are. Those of us who are working. The congress can't wait to take our earnings for themselves. And this is not a one party spending spree. Members of both parties have enjoyed the longevity in office and prosperity they get from reaching into your pockets.

When welfare gifts are given to those who will not go to school or go to work, some in congress gain from the votes and contributions it brings them. And when your taxes are given to the giants of industry in the form of subsidies, trade deals, government contracts or tax breaks some in congress gain from the votes and contributions it brings them. We must not forget the immeasurable cost and suffering lived by the victims of welfare induced crime.

Whether it's Rape, Pillage, Robbery or Murder the victim's suffering never ends. The medical and emotional trauma caused by welfare crimes, whether due to the use of drugs and alcohol or lack of conscience, leaves the victims who survive with a lifetime of heart wrenching sorrow. And it ends the opportunity to live, grow and prosper for those victims whose lives are cut short. And don't forget the people who are victimized by government taking their earnings. It robs them of the ability to build a better life for their families and educate their children.

The great vote spending spree congress entered into once they had the power to tax your earnings led to the great society, the fair deal and the new deal. But by whatever name you call it, it is a raw deal for working Americans. The cost in taxes to working

Americans for this government sponsored welfare is in the hundreds of billions now, and if continued it will climb to trillions of dollars each year. But the cost in dollars for today's workers is nothing compared to the cost our children and grandchildren will pay if the current crop of socialist in congress have their way.

Our forefathers warned us about uncontrolled taxation and entering into treaties with foreign states. Disregarding the warnings of our forefathers the congress has supported so called treaties with groups of foreign states that obligate America to use our economic strength and military forces to suppress so called civil wars in those states.

Whether it be Korea, Viet Nam, Bosnia, Haiti, Viet Nam or wherever the results have been the same. Our government interfered in the affairs of other nations at a terrible cost to America in lives and tax dollars. We fought a forty year cold war that cost American taxpayers four trillion dollars in taxes. Russia did not then, and has never, had the economic strength or military might to challenge America in a full scale war. But the Military industrialists made fortunes during that cold war, and American tax payers paid the bills.

Ignoring the warnings of our fathers, Washington started on a free wheeling spending spree at the close of world war two that continues to expand and grow with each passing year. First we rebuilt the countries and economies of the nations we defeated and those we defended. We rebuilt Japan and China to the point where they out produce America today. We left three hundred thousand military personnel and equipment in Germany where they still remain today. We pay the state of Germany an annual fortune to let us keep them there, and those service members and their dependents spend their earnings in Germany supporting their economy.

We have military personnel in Korea, Japan, Bosnia and more than one hundred other countries around the world at a terrible expense to American taxpayers. Following world war two Washington, erroneously believed they could buy loyalty and friendship, so they started a program called foreign aid. I suppose they believed they could purchase the friendship and loyalty of others like they do in the political world of Washington. But any honest working person knows you can't buy friendship, what you do is start a program of giving that never ends.

Did the thousands of soldiers and billions they spend in Germany persuade them to support us in Korea, Viet Nam or Iraq? Did the thousands of soldiers and the billions we give to the mid-east countries and Europe persuade them to support America in Korea, Viet Nam or Iraq? Was there any country we sent our forces into in so called conflicts to save democracy any better off than they were before we invaded their countries?

North Korea is a nuclear armed communist state, Viet Nam is a Communist country. Iraq is engaged in a continuation of the civil war they have been engaged in for more than four thousand years.

When taxes from working Americans were used to put the Shaw of Iran into power in Iran, were the Iranian people any better off? When billions more was used to keep him in power were the people any better off? Is America any safer today than before the Shaw was placed in power with our taxes? The answer is no. Iran is now a state led by a dictator who hates America and American taxpayers. Iran is where they were before the Shaw, an Islamic state, except they now are developing the nuclear bomb they can use on our friends or threaten us to get their way.

Today, Washington takes hundreds of billions of tax dollars from working Americans, then gives those tax dollars to a hundred countries around the world. Most of what Washington calls foreign aid is nothing but gifts to wealthy rulers, for it never reaches the people in those countries. And it doesn't buy loyalty, one look at crude oil prices confirms that the billions in aid Washington gives the kings, princes and sheiks of oil producing states hasn't lowered the cost we pay them for their oil one cent. But so what, Socialist Washington money comes out of the pockets of American workers, not out of the politicians inflated pockets.

Under agreements with the United Nations Washington spends hundreds of billions in foreign states for so called medical aid. A hundred billion alone just for African states to supposedly control the aids epidemic. Instead of telling the people in those states living and breeding like animals is causing their aids problems, Washington spends billions of our tax dollars treating them for their self induced diseases. This is just one example of where your earnings are going to waste, and Washington is giving your earnings away all around the world for United Nations sponsored programs.

Now congress is attempting to enact programs to legalize the invasion coming across our borders. They have already rewarded twenty million of the criminal invaders with amnesty and are working to adopt legislation that will reward another ten to twenty million.

These criminals are rewarded not only by granting them amnesty, but by furnishing them a free education for their children, housing assistance for them and their children, and free medical care and medications. As their numbers grow by illegally entering our country to get government amnesty and handouts, the number of their offspring increase just as drastically.

Today American taxpayers have had their income taxes, social security taxes, Medicare taxes and Medicaid taxes drastically increased just to provide hundreds of billions of dollars each year to criminal immigrants and their offspring. Hundreds of billions of tax dollars are used to furnish Housing, medical care, education, welfare and hundreds of billions more to cover the cost of furnishing the comforts of home for those criminal invaders who are caught and imprisoned for killing, looting and raping American citizens, and bringing their poisonous drugs across our borders.

The United Nations agreements that require us to provide legal and civil protection to criminal immigrants crossing our borders will encourage forty million more to illegally enter our country. And the predictable increase in welfare rolls will add a terrible tax cost to working Americans. The cost of trying to reduce the inflow of illegal drugs across the borders and reduce the rising violence they cause will strain the budgets of every working American. But it will buy votes for the liberals and socialists in Washington. Liberals and socialists of both political parties will give America away to secure the illegal votes of these criminals.

It is interesting to note: during the period 1940 to 1960, before the advent of welfare, the poverty rate among African American families dropped from 87 percent to 47 percent. That was nearly a fifty percent reduction during that period. This suggests that poverty rates would have continued to fall had the Great Society War on Poverty not been started. But the votes were there, ready for the next purchase price, paid in welfare giveaways of every type and description.

Clearly anyone, regardless of race, sex or ancestry will stop going to school and working once they find government will provide for them if they don't want to or have to help themselves.

Helping those who because of mental or physical conditions are unable to help themselves is one thing, but forcing working taxpayers to provide for those who would take a handout rather than work is another matter. It is Socialism. It is purchasing voter support with your taxed earnings.

Our congress and our presidents have betrayed us. They have reduced our ability to save from our earnings because what could have been savings are now taken by Washington in taxes. They will cater to those who would rather vote for a handout than work for a living. Make no mistake about it. They will trade your children's future for your vote today. They will trade your children's freedom for your vote today. They will trade your children's liberty for your vote today. They will sell our national sovereignty tomorrow for your vote today.

Every working family in America are forced to balance their family budget. And to try to do so after Washington steals one half their earnings is impossible. As the result, many lose their homes and go to bed hungry while Washington spends and wastes their earnings.

The people should demand Washington balance the federal budget. And demand they do so by reducing spending, not by increasing taxes. Unless the people fight to keep their earnings Washington will never stop taking their earnings and wasting it to appease the United Nations or buy votes and corporate loyalty.

I can think of no words of advice more appropriate for those who look for a free handout than the words of Samuel Adams, " If ye love welfare better than liberty, the tranquility of servitude better than freedom, crouch down and lick the hands of those who feed you. May your chains set lightly upon you. May posterity forget that ye were our countrymen".

Joining The United Nations

The third step taken by Washington that will lead to the collapse of America was becoming a member state of the Socialist organized and Socialist run United Nations. That step started America on the road to the loss of American independence and national sovereignty.

The name itself, United Nations, implies that a world government is more desirable and sustainable than one country, our United States. The term, United Nations, was first coined by United States President Franklin D. Roosevelt. It was first used in the "declaration by the United Nations" of 1 January 1942. That was during the Second World War when representatives of twenty six nations pledged their governments to continue fighting together against the Axis Powers.

I would remind the people that joining together as individual states to fight a common enemy is one thing. But forming a United Nations, a New World Order as former president George Bush so lovingly called it, wherein all the peoples of the world are subject to the laws created by a self appointed few is another thing entirely. Especially when those United Nations are led by Socialists and Communists who are sworn enemies of the United States and the American people.

The forerunner of the United Nations was the League of Nations, an organization conceived in similar circumstances during the first world war. It was established in the year 1919 under the treaty of Versailles to promote international cooperation and to achieve peace and security. That organization ceased to exist after failing to prevent the second world war. Perhaps our leaders in Washington should have studied history before organizing and joining the current attempt at world government. But apparently they did not, or they chose to ignore the lessons of history.

In 1945 representatives of fifty countries met in San Francisco at the United Nations Conference on international organization to draw up the United Nations Charter. Those delegates deliberated on the basis of proposals worked out in 1944 by (of all people) representatives from China, the Soviet Union, The United Kingdom and the United States. The charter was signed on 26 June 1945 by the representatives of fifty countries.

I believe a review of the articles of just one chapter of the United Nations Charter adopted in 1945, Chapter seven, tells exactly what the goals of the communist and socialists who rule the United Nations are. Chapter seven spells out the powers and authorities of The United Nations Security Council, with respect to actions the United Nations may take to forces other states to comply with United Nations world policies. I believe a review of this one chapter of their charter clearly shows the intentions and goals of the unelected Socialists and Communists who run the United Nations is World Rule.

Chapter Seven of the United Nations charter describes the authorities and actions the United Nations shall take with respect to threats to the peace, or breaches of the peace, and acts of aggression towards United Nations member states. Note: this clearly demonstrates the self appointed leaders of the United Nations are concerned only with threats to their rule, not threats to the peace and stability of other countries. And the record of United Nations economic sanctions and military actions confirm that.

Article 39 states; The Security Council shall determine the existence of any threat to the peace, breach of peace, or act of aggression towards another United Nations member state, and shall decide what measures shall be taken in accordance with articles 41 and 42, to maintain or restore international peace and security. (Note; the United Nations Security Council shall decide when there has been a breach of peace, and what action is in their best interests. Not the interests of the American people or the free world.)

Article 40 states; In order to prevent an aggravation of a situation the security council may call upon the parties concerned, to comply with such provisional measures it deems necessary or desirable. The security council shall duly take account of failure to comply with such provisional measures. (In plain language, if we or any other country fails to live up to United Nations rules or demands, they will remember our failure to do so and hold it against us). Does this sound like a threat to you, do as we say or else?

Article 41 states; The security council may decide what provisional measures not involving the use of armed forces are to be employed to give effect to its decisions. And it may call upon the members of the United Nations to apply such measures. These may include complete or partial interruption of economic relations and of rail, sea, air, postal, radio, telegraphic and other means of communication, and the severance of diplomatic relations.

(Note, every time the United Nations has called upon it's member states, it has been American forces that were called into action to enforce United Nations sanctions and military action. Policies that have sent us into war in Korea, Viet Nam, Bosnia, Somalia and a dozen other states.)

When is Washington going to learn that we have no business being the military enforcement arm of the United Nations? Do we really want to give control of our armed forces to the United Nations any time they call? Is it not a violation of our constitution to give a foreign ruler control of our military forces? I ask you: Are your leaders in Washington serving you, or the New World Order?

Article 42 states; Should the security council decide that measures provided for in article 41 would be inadequate, or have proved to be inadequate, it may take such action by air, sea, or land forces as may be necessary to maintain or restore international peace and security. Such action may include demonstrations, blockades and other operations by land, sea and air forces of the United Nations.

Does this sound like a threat, do it our way or face military action? And remember, every time the United Nations leaders have decided to use military action it has been American military forces and finances that are used.

Article 43 states; All members of the United Nations, in order to contribute to the maintenance of international peace and security, shall undertake to make available to the security council, on it's call and in accordance with a special agreement or agreements, armed forces, assistance, facilities, including rights of passage necessary for the purpose of maintaining international peace and security.

Such agreements shall govern the numbers and types of forces, their state of readiness and general location, and the nature of the facilities and assistance to be provided. (Did you know Washington agreed to keep our military forces available, in a state of readiness, for the United Nations and open our facilities and give rights of passage thru America to that Socialist organization)? Could that be the reason we don't have enough soldiers to police our borders or fight in Iraq and Afghanistan?

Article 45 states; In order to enable the United Nations to take urgent military measures, members shall hold immediately available their air force contingents for combined international action. The strength and degree of readiness of these contingents and plans for their combined action shall be determined within the limits laid down in the special agreement or agreements referred to in Article 43, by the security council with the assistance of the Military Staff Committee. Note, America is not a member of the United Nations military staff and we no longer have veto power over the security council decisions. United Nations socialist and communist leaders have cleverly organized their leadership so we no longer have a vote on any military action ordered by the security council.

Article 47, section 1: There shall be established a military staff committee to advise and assist the security council on all questions related to the security council's military requirements for the employment and command of forces placed at it's disposal, the regulations of armaments, and possible disarmament.

(Note, They decide what military requirements they need from America, and they command and employ our forces.) Did your sons and daughters know they might be serving under United Nations commanders when they enlisted? Is this not a direct violation of our national constitution?

Section 2; The military staff committee shall consist of the chiefs of staff of the permanent members of the security council or their representatives. Any member of the United Nations not permanently represented on the committee shall be invited by the committee to be associated with it, but only when the efficient discharge of committee responsibilities require the participation of that member.

Section 3; The military staff committee shall be responsible under the security council for the strategic direction of any armed forces placed at the disposal of the security council. Questions relating to the command of such forces shall be worked out subsequently. Note; the United Nations Security Council established the military staff command, and they decide who commands it, and what kind and amount of military actions to take. (In other words they will decide what military actions to take and who commands our forces after we provide them, And since we no longer have a veto vote in the security council where does that put our military forces? Under the command of United Nations commanders)

I believe you will agree this one Article, and it's various sections, clearly leaves it up to the United Nations as to when and where to use military force, what forces we will supply them, what they will be used for and who will command them. Is this what you want, a bunch of communists and socialists and Moslem leaders controlling our military forces?

Consider what Article 48 of the United Nations charter says. Item 1. The actions required to carry out the decisions of the security council for the maintenance of international peace and security shall be taken by all members of the United Nations or by some of them, as the security council decides. (Again they make the decisions with or without our participation, and we no longer have a veto vote.)

Chapter V11 is just a small section of the United Nations charter. But it should be enough to convince anyone that we have been betrayed by Washington. They have sold us out. They have sold out our military service members. Apparently the United Nations charter and the Socialists and Communists who control that organization mean more to the socialist leaders in Washington than the people of America and our constitution does.

Possibly if we review exactly how The United Nations officially came into existence, and who participated in organizing that Unholy Alliance, we would better understand the real purpose of it's organizers. The United Nations officially came into existence on 24 October 1945, when it was ratified by China, France, The Soviet Union, The United Kingdom, The United States and a number of other countries. With that beginning, The third step to the collapse of American independence was officially and permanently set in place.

It was no accident that the United Nations headquarters was located in America. The socialist membership of the Council on Foreign Relations worked with their fellow socialists in Washington to bring the United Nations to America. A party of Socialists who have one goal, a socialistic world government.

The United Nations Headquarters consists of four main buildings: the secretariat, the general assembly, the conference area and the library. Construction started on October 24th 1949 at a cost of sixty five million.

Remember, sixty five million in 1949 is about approximate to three hundred sixty five billion today. The financing of the United Nations Headquarters was provided by the United States as an interest free loan. But remember, your taxes provided the financing for that loan. It is claimed that loan was repaid however, do you know of anyone who were returned the taxes taken from them to fund this Socialistic Communistic headquarters on American soil?

The cost of remodeling and expansions have added hundreds of millions more to the cost of the buildings and grounds and the cost of continuing the United Nations programs are astronomical. All member states are legally obliged to pay a share of the costs of this New World Order headquarters. The top provider, under the formula worked out by member states, is of course the United States. However, other member states owed billions in current and past operations as of January 2006. And the American worker sees their earnings taxes steadily increased to make up for that deficit.

The costs for keeping all of the hundreds of committees and their worldwide policies and actions going is in the hundreds of billions of dollars. Those costs also are supposed to be shared by all member states. But the other United Nations member states do not meet their obligations which means your taxes are increased to make up the deficits.

To this 18 acre tract comes representatives from the earths six billion people, to discuss and decide issues of peace and justice (international law style), and matters of economic and social well being. Lest we forget, why should your taxes be wasted letting the leaders of a socialist organization decide issues of peace or justice.

Not one leader ever elected or appointed to hold the position of United Nations presidency, or any of it's commissions ever lived in, ruled over or led a nation of democratic people. We should not forget that, ninety percent of the worlds population and their representatives, who come to the United Nations compound, are mostly Moslem and Communist and Socialists and are enemies of America and any who hold to the Christian faith.

I have to question their abilities and knowledge about democracy, or their meaning of world peace and justice. None of the leaders and almost no member states have lived in a free constitutionally governed country. American workers are literally being taxed to pay the cost of destroying our national heritage, our national sovereignty and our Christian faith. Our taxes are being used to further the goals of anti American socialists and communist leaders of the United Nations.

With a controlled press and media few citizens realize that Americas membership in the United Nations poses a very real threat to our survival as a free sovereign nation. Here are some reasons why you should be more than concerned. Why you should be ready to march on Washington and demand we withdraw our membership from that Totalitarian New World Order.

The United Nations basic philosophy is anti-American, anti-Christian and pro-Totalitarian. Consider this, Our Declaration of Independence proclaims the "self evident truth men are endowed by their creator with certain unalienable rights". But in it's covenant the United Nations ignores God's existence and implies that the United Nations grants rights, and then repeatedly claims the power , as provided by the United Nations charter, to cancel all individual citizens rights out of existence. In fact, the United Nations charter makes it a crime under international law for parents to require their children to attend religious services. Does that sound like the kind of government you want your children enslaved under?

How many people know The United Nations was founded and organized by Communists and the Council on Foreign Relations members whose common goal is a socialist world government. Sixteen Key United States officials who shaped the policies leading to the creation of the United Nations were later exposed as Communists. These included, Alger Hiss, chief planner of the 1945 founding conference, and assistant Secretary of Treasurer

Harry Dexter White. And that goal has never changed. United Nations leaders today are more determined than ever to destroy America and replace it with an anti-Christian, anti-democratic nation under the control of the United Nations.

Since it's beginning, the Council on Foreign Relations (CFR) has always worked for world government. The key Council on Foreign Relations founder, Edward House, in his book "Philip Dru" called for Socialism as dreamed of by Karl Marx. Forty three (43) members of the United States delegation at the United Nations founding conference in 1945 were or would become Council on Foreign Relations members.

These are the people who organized the great betrayal, our leaders in Washington selected them, so what do you believe their real goals are.

The United Nations has always chosen socialist and communists for leaders. The first Secretary General was Soviet Spy Alger Hiss. He was followed by Norwegian socialist, Trygve Lie. Then came Swedish socialist Dag Hammarskjold, Burmese Marxist U Thant, former Austrian Nazi Kurt Waldheim, Peruvian socialist Javier Perez Decuellar and Egyptian socialist Boutros Ghali. Each used the full resources of the United Nations to promote communism and further their socialist causes.

The socialist international party (which proudly traces it's origin to the first international socialist party headed by Karl Marx), today claims tens of millions of members in fifty four countries. Almost all of the United Nations " independent commissions" for the last thirty years have been members of the socialist international party. This organization has declared their objective is nothing less than world government. They believe membership in the United Nations must be made universal. Yet the first president Bush and others who followed him often speak with great fondness for the New World Order.

The United Nations is building it's own army to enforce it's will upon the world. This plan adopted by the security council in 1992 called, an agenda for peace, calls for armed forces of member states (of which the United States is one) to be made permanently available to the United Nations. This United Nations agenda for peace claims, " the time for individual states to have national constitutions and national sovereignty has passed. Washington agreed, and became the United Nations world peacekeeping force. Since then Washington has furnished military forces, and financing, for United Nations incursions into dozens of countries. These include Korea, Viet Nam, Bosnia, Haiti, Somalia, Afghanistan and Iraq just to name a few.

Chapter V11, of the United Nations charter states, when sanctions or boycotts fail to force a country to accept United Nations dictates; land, sea, and air forces can be used to enforce United Nations international law. And every time this charter provision has been used to coerce a state into compliance with United Nations laws it has been American soldiers who fought and died in those no win United Nations wars.

In accordance with Chapter V11 of the United Nations charter, United States policies and our military forces are enforcing United Nations laws and your taxes are paying the cost for this United Nations army. In a number of United Nations ordered conflicts Foreign United Nations commanders have commanded our troops. This is a direct violation of our constitution that gives only our Congress the right to declare war. We have even seen United States military officers face military courts martial's for refusing to wear United Nations uniforms or serve under United Nations commanders. Another direct violation of our constitution and a violation of the Universal Military Code of Justice, The law governing our military forces. Our military personnel take an oath to serve our country, defend our constitution, not the United Nations Charter.

Incredibly, it has been the official policy of the United States government since 1961, to disarm America and create a United Nations army. This policy concludes; progressive controlled disarmament, of all nations including the United States, would proceed to the point where no nation would have the power to challenge the United Nations armies. (See state department publication 7277: Freedom from war). Were the American people ever advised of this agreement that will lead to the disarmament of America, including privately owned firearms by American citizens.

Thousands of US military personnel have lost their lives in places like Haiti, Somalia, Yugoslavia, Lebanon, Pakistan, Iraq and a dozen other small states while serving under United Nations commands. One might ask, why has the United Nations refused and failed to act to liberate the people of oppressed nations under Communist or Socialist rule.

When Soviet armies invaded Hungary in the 1950's, when the Chinese invaded Tibet in the 1960's, When the Soviets invaded Afghanistan in the 1970's and When Russia invaded Chechnya in the 1990's the United Nations did nothing.

But the United Nations declared tiny Rhodesia a threat to international peace then enabled pro communist Robert Mugabe to seize power. And it was the United Nations led military force that brought the self described communist Nelson Mandela to power. I ask you, are those countries any better off than they were before the United Nations invaded their countries?

In 1949 anti-communist Nationalist China, a founding member of the United Nations, was forced from the China mainland by the Communist, and settled in Taiwan. In 1971 the United Nations expelled Taiwan, a founding member of the United Nations, then embraced the brutal Communist Chinese government in China. That Chinese Communist government was responsible for the murders of more than 35 million people. But the United Nations delegates were overjoyed that the United Nations had thrown out the United Sates backed Taiwan government and admitted Communist Red China. This is the New World Order the Socialists in Washington would have you turn your lives and families over to.

America supplies the money and military power while the United Nations finances tyrants and assorted enemies of the

United States. American workers taxes pay twenty five percent of the total United Nations budget plus thirty one percent of all United Nations special agency budgets. Taxes collected from American workers also provide billions more to the International Monetary Fund, The World Bank and other agencies created by, and used for, United Nations projects that subvert the American economy. These funds went to Marxist dictator Mengistu in Ethiopia, Tanzanian dictator Julius Nyerere and to the Vietnam Communist after American forces fled Vietnam.

Sixty thousand American service members lost their lives in that United Nations sponsored conflict. And that doesn't count the thousands upon thousands who suffered and died from the effects of killer herbicides, now known as agent orange, sprayed upon our service members by our own government while serving in Viet Nam. And don't forget the hundreds of thousands more who came home physically and emotionally scarred for life, to face the scorn of their countrymen and neglect from their government. And the granite wall in Arlington can never make restitution to the millions of military veterans who came home from Viet Nam to wander the streets emotionally scarred, physically destroyed and forgotten.

The United Nations claims to be a world peace organization. It is not, it is a war organization. Article 42 of the United Nations charter states, they have the authority to use air, sea, and land forces to force other states to submit to United Nations authority. The United Nations will use whatever military might and technological weapons the United States provides them to force all nations of the world to submit to United Nations rule. Remember, Washington agreed with chapter V11 of the United Nations charter that requires us to furnish that organization military forces and technology whenever they ask or demand it. They will intentionally drain the United States of all financial and military resources to insure when the moment arrives to require our nation to submit to total United Nations authority, America will not have the military or financial resources to resist.

Our government has already agreed to the 1992 United Nations agenda for peace policies that require us to abolish the sovereignty of America and become an enslaved people under the control of the Communist and Socialists who rule the United Nations. It was not expected to be accomplished overnight. America was a nation of strong willed Christian people.

They were the most industrious people ever to inhabit the earth God gave them. America would have to be dismantled one step at a time to keep the people unaware of their coming fate. Each policy or treaty adopted by the United Nations is a step towards hastening the collapse of America.

Obtain a listing of all United Nations past presidents and Secretary Generals and heads of the Security Council. Check the names of all those who have been given authority over the various committees assembled by the United Nations. You will not find the name of one person from the countries of, Great Britain, Australia or the United States of America, or any other country considered to have a democratic form of government. And so it will be when the United Nations finally gains control over America. No American, unless they be members of the Council on Foreign Relations, will ever be appointed to rule over the American people, preside over the United Nations Security Council, the United Nations General Assembly or any of it's numerous agencies or committees.

The Communists and Socialists are determined to bring America into submission to the power of the United Nations. Submission on their terms where America will have no real voice in the decisions made by the United Nations Security Council or General Assembly. They have already stripped America of it's veto power in United Nations voting procedures. The United Nations will rule America and the American people will have no voice in the decisions made.

As recently as December 2007 the United Nations general assembly issued a resolution that states; America must keep it's forces in Iraq. This at a time when many have come to question our purpose of being there. One is forced to ask whether the socialists and atheists in Washington are serving the American people or the United Nations. And when one studies their records and policies it isn't hard to see their loyalties lie with the United Nations.

Our forefathers warned us about the dangers of entering into treaties with foreign nations. They cautioned us that doing so would lead to wars. They warned us never to give the federal government the power to tax the people. Our leaders ignored those warnings and today the American people are the heaviest taxed people in the world, and we are the most militarily involved nation since the beginning of recorded history.

The people of America are also to blame for the current dismal state of affairs in America. Their apathy and malaise left them indifferent to the policies of the Washington corrupt. America has become so addicted to watching the nakedness and pornography on the socialists controlled media and in the films coming out of Hollywood they are indifferent to the changes taking place in Washington and around America.

Three generations of teaching our children they are the descendents of animals while prohibiting any mention or discussions regarding their Biblical creation worked. The older generations have or are departing this life leaving behind three generations of citizens who are so engrossed in having fun they are unaware of the changes taking place in American government and it's policies.

It is said that Nero fiddled while Rome burned. Unless the people of America wake up, take their government back, history will record that the people of America watched the filth while America collapsed. The clock is ticking and the hour is growing late for all America. This step has been completed we have been sold out to the United Nations. Only an informed, loyal and courageous people can stop the clock and prevent Washington from taking the next step towards collapse.

CREATING A CONTROLLED MEDIA

The next step leading to the collapse of America was controlling the media and press. Hitler, Stalin and all brutal would be world rulers knew, controlling what the people are told is the most important action necessary to gain control over the people. The socialists in Washington, and those behind the scenes, know that controlling what the people are told about the United Nations, and the United Nations treaties Washington became partner too, was an absolute necessity if the people were going to be sold on the idea of a one world government.

In the years that followed the formation of the United Nations, more than five hundred multilateral treaties with member states were adopted by the Communist and Socialist leaders in the United Nations. Washington became partners in many of those treaties without the knowledge of, or more important, the advised consent of the American people. It was feared that the American people would not look favorable upon the United Nations policies if they were aware of the backgrounds and political beliefs of those leaders who control that Socialist organization.

Socialist Liberals and Conservative Republicans in Washington were having a great time taxing and spending the working families earnings. At the same time they were slowly turning more control of American policies, finances and military capacity over to the United Nations. Becoming a member of the United Nations was sold to America as strengthening the worlds ability to fight off radical states that threaten the worlds democracies. But the leaders of the New World Order are demanding more military and financial support from America and using those resources to eliminate any state that refuses to buckle under to United Nations policies.

A way had to be found to avoid the public learning the extent and truth about Washington's agreements with and support of the United Nations. A controlled media was the answer. Monopoly laws were changed to permit individual or corporate ownership of large segments of the media.

Monopoly laws were changed to allow large segments of the press to be owned by foreign interests. Television medias were also now controlled by large corporate interests. The owners and executives of these corporate media outlets were liberals indebted to Washington and more than willing to promote the socialist agenda of Washington.

The driving force behind all United Nations policies is the destruction of the sovereignty of the United States and enslavement of the American people under the control of the one world government. The vast majority of the American people are totally unaware of the dangers they face as member states within the United Nations World Order. The reason for this is because those who were controlling the news are very good at it. The State Department, the military spokespersons, the Congress and the white house became very good at controlling what the press and media were told, and what they reported. Because of this the people, out of ignorance, apathetically accepted the idea that a new world order would be a good thing for America.

Some citizens circulated petitions containing hundreds of thousands of signatures of citizens demanding America withdraw from the United Nations, and reject all treaties previously agreed with. But the voice of the people was ignored by the New World Order supporters in Washington. The reporting of those petitioners voices were not even reported by the media. In the year 2008, one member of the congress proposed legislation that would have cut off all funding and support for the United Nations and it's numerous committees, but that legislation went nowhere. Because his proposed legislation was never reported by the media or taken to committee for a vote by the legislature. The controlled press prevented the people from even hearing about the proposal.

Washington was slowly following the path taken by totalitarian governments in other countries who had controlled their people by controlling what they were allowed to see, speak or hear. At the same time opposing voices were being silenced, the major media outlets continued their praise of the United Nations , it's leaders, and their supporters in Washington.

We now have a senate legislator, a candidate for president, proposing private government sponsored schools. Taxpayers will be forced to give more of their earnings to pay the cost of these schools should they come into being. The purpose of these proposed schools was said to be to teach and instruct young citizens how to become public service workers. But remember, what Washington legislators promise compared to what they do, seldom are the same.

To some the idea of youth camps bring back memories of the Hitler and Stalin youth camps, where the young were indoctrinated into believing in, and following the orders of, their leaders. There were some who feared such a program may lead to our own American Gestapo units or KGB units, enforcing the orders of their leaders. But there was no mention or discussion of the proposed training schools by the media. The people were so mired in their apathy they never heard of or considered the dangers of the proposed indoctrination centers.

When Washington legislators decided to institute globalization foreign policies to comply with the United Nations General Agreement on Tariffs and Trade (GATT) policies they commenced a concentrated propaganda campaign to convince the people American workers would benefit from global markets. Briefings from the state department and congress were released to the media and Corporate America were running their own advertisement campaigns. But there was a far more sinister purpose behind globalization. Sadly the American people never heard the other side of globalization until it was too late.

The controlled media was used to insure the liberals and Socialists running for election or reelection to the office of presidency or federal legislative positions did not have to answer for their records, or have their records questioned over the media by any opposition candidate or the people. Consider the McCain-Feingold campaign finance law. That law prohibits the common people from pooling their financial resources in order to get their voices heard sixty days prior to an election.

Yet it places no limits on the amount of financial resources a Socialist billionaire, American or foreigner, can spend prior to an election. Nor does it appear to limit the amount of time the media can spend supporting their socialists candidates prior to an election.

That law appears to have been adopted primarily to silence the National Rifle Association, and prevent them from reporting the voting records of the anti-gun Liberals and Socialists. But it was also aimed at silencing any organized opposition to globalization policies. That campaign finance law probably did more than any other policy to insure the reelection of liberal incumbents and candidates who support the New World Order and globalization trade policies.

Why is it the media never mentions the Chinese financial contributions to Liberal candidates who have held and are running for the office of the presidency? Why have they not mentioned the millions in financial contributions made by Moslem people living in foreign countries? Nor do they mention the millions contributed to their liberal candidates by billionaire foreign controlled media move on organizations. The controlled media can promote their own liberal agenda and campaign for their candidates with biased and even fabrications, right up to the day of scheduled elections. But citizens are prohibited by the McCain Feingold law from combining their resources to promote the truth sixty days prior to elections.

As recently as December 2007 the congress revised monopoly laws to allow socialist controlled newspapers to also take over (own) the television media covering the same areas as their newspapers. This will insure the same biased views are published in print as voiced over the airwaves and thereby eliminating all opposing viewpoints. Few people ever heard of this change in monopoly laws because the liberal socialist media did not report it.

Have you heard the media report on the latest anti-American, anti-Democratic policy started by Russia, a member of the United Nations? As recently as 24 December 2007 Russia announced it would start providing their state of the ark anti missile defense system to Iran. A system far more effective than anything we have. That was followed by their decision to start sending submarines to the Iranian government. The only purpose for which would be to assist Iran should America decide to move against their Nuclear Bomb program they intend to use against Israel.

As it was with Hitler and Stalin when the people were told only what the dictators wanted them to hear, so it is becoming in America today. Our forefathers warned , Be wary of any who threaten your right to speak, the right of a free people to assemble and voice their opinion lest we lose that right. We have accepted a media system in which all media speaks with the same voice, the voice of the liberal socialists in Washington. We have accepted the Washington laws and lost our right to unite and speak as one prior to an election.

Today the socialist Anti-Christ media has all but banned any mention of Christ during the Christmas season by their commentators. Yet at the same time every television program and every movie coming out of Hollywood are filled with nakedness, sex and violence of every kind and description. These liberal Programs are directed towards destroying our Christian heritage. There only purpose is to keep the people so occupied with watching these filthy productions they will not be aware of the direction Washington is taking America.

There is only one media, actually a small part of one media, talk radio, where an opposing voice can sometimes be heard. But that media is under attack from all directions. Those who speak other than the way the Washington socialist and media socialist are finding their jobs threatened by every means possible. Even on the floors of congress their names are vilified. One can only describe the major media today as a controlled media. An arm of the liberal socialist movement.

Today, anyone who dares to disagree with the socialist agenda in Washington are considered to be radicals, so I have no doubt if this book is published and becomes known, there will be some who will accuse me of being a radical. But the fact is, speaking the truth is considered radical today. Sadly, Americans have kept silent out of fear and allowed apathy to rule their hearts and minds. That apathy has allowed the socialist in our midst to corrupt the media with their socialists views.

The media today is a controlled media. Controlled by the socialist who want a one world government with them in control. It became that way with the aid of government officials and the policies they have instituted. It became so in order to impose the views of the New World Order upon the American people without their knowledge or understanding of where Washington was leading them. A person cannot watch television without seeing the faces of liberal candidates, and hear the glowing reports about their self proclaimed accomplishments.

Our apathy and malaise has dishonored our forefathers. Time is running out for those who love freedom. One more step necessary to insure the collapse of America has been taken, with only a few steps remaining before collapse will occur.

Destroying Our Industrial Base

The next step taken by Washington leading to the collapse of America was to betray the American people by destroying the industrial base and manufacturing capability of America. Giving foreign countries our industrial technology. This chapter describes those policies already completed and others underway. It provides a description of how these globalization policies have and will affect the American labor movement. Finally in this chapter we see the predictable final outcome of globalization policies, instituted by the leaders of the United Nations and adopted by Washington.

Globalization started with the 1994 adoption of the General Agreement on Tariffs and Trade (GATT) by the United Nations. An agreement Washington was partner to. Former House Speaker Newt Gingrich warned the congress and administration that the GATT treaty would transfer a significant authority on trade and tariff policies to the United Nations. He likened it to the Maastricht treaty that required European states to surrender most of their sovereignty. GATT gives the United Nations control over international trade and tariffs, and eventually the authority to impose an income tax on the citizens of all member states. Including all American workers.

Globalization it was called, and sold by Washington and the controlled media, as the next great industrial revolution in America. It would open up the world markets for American made goods and products. It would bring millions of new high tech jobs to America they claimed. One person Ross Perot, a candidate for office of the presidency also spoke out. He tried to convince the people globalization would destroy America, but the people failed to heed his words and elected a socialist to hold that office, and the great globalization effort was underway.

Within a few years after the ratification of the United Nations General Agreement on Trade and Tariffs (GATT) American workers began to see the real purpose and results of globalization. American Corporations began the transfer of their operations overseas, primarily to China at first, a historically proven Communist nation. Before long the Chinese economy was booming with the immense building and equipping of factories. Preparing them to produce all the products formerly made by American workers. Televisions, radios, VCRs, textiles, automobiles and spare parts and thousands of other products now being manufactured in America.

Once these factories were completed in Asia and around the world American corporations then equipped these Asian countries with the tools and machinery necessary to go into production. At the same time this was happening our industries were being used here at home to teach and train foreign workers how to set up and operate the equipment we furnished them. Much of that cost was paid with your taxes on government contracts with industry. As these workers, engineers, tool and die makers, aircraft engine assemblers, and operations managers became proficient they returned to their countries. There they started to work, at slave wages, manufacturing and assembling products formerly made in America by American workers. I say formerly because American industries were shut down once foreign industries became operational, and millions of Americans were unemployed and displaced.

Aircraft engine assembly plants were placed into operation in Turkey, Japan and France. Once these installations were operational tens of thousands of aircraft workers in America found themselves out of work. Then steel mills, fabrication plants, automobile manufacturers, tool and die makers, production machine builders, aircraft engine plants, manufacturing and assembly plants for every product formerly made in America were set into operation in Europe, Asia and Japan.

Once these factories became operational American industries closed their doors forever. American workers found themselves facing unemployment and foreclosures on their homes and automobiles.

Even the weapons our military services use, their firearms and ammunition, were being manufactured overseas. The guidance systems for some of our long range missiles were now being manufactured and assembled in Asia. We can only wonder whether these systems have had installed in them a program to turn them around on command, and send them back to where they came from, if they were ever used. American corporation profits rose as they obtained cheap foreign products made by slave workers. Corporate profits increased even more when the congress reduced corporate taxes and even eliminated corporate taxes on some companies doing business out of the country.

With corporate taxes eliminated on products being made overseas by cheap slave labor their profits increased even more. But former American workers did not share in those profits, they had lost their jobs. They had been replaced by Japanese, Chinese, Turkish, French, Brazilian and other workers around the world.

Once these offshore plants were operational, globalization came home to America. Globalization came to America in the form of closed factories, closed plants, closed steel mills and all the other industries that comprised the steel, automotive, caterpillar factories and Jet engine assembly plants. Manufacturing production machines, and tool and die manufacturers and hundreds of other industrial plants were closed for good. And globalization came home to America in the form of millions of unemployed American workers and long unemployment and welfare lines. The propaganda put out by Washington and their controlled media was right. Globalization would create millions of jobs. But it would not create jobs in America, it eliminated them.

Millions of American jobs were lost forever due to these offshore moves to the Asian continent. And millions of American workers found themselves unemployed and forced to work for substandard wages in service industries or, were reduced to standing in welfare and unemployment lines. Many millions lost their homes and were forced to exist with their families in the alleys and shadows of society. The construction of homeless shelters, payday cash outlets, pawn shops and temporary employment agencies were the only businesses booming in America. America was fast becoming a third world country with all hope for the future lost.

The second phase of globalization followed soon afterwards. Many American accounting, auditing, Book-keeping, credit card banking industries, and collection agencies moved their operations to Asia, primarily to India, where they could get these services performed by low paid workers. Before long when the people called a number for information they found it was answered from somewhere in India. Again, millions of former American workers found themselves standing in welfare and unemployment lines. And again, many millions more lost their homes and were forced to exist in the alleys and shadows of society.

The next phase saw American retail giants move their procurement offices to Asia. There goods and products such as clothing garments, shoes, toys, household products, sweepers, television sets, recording machines and playing devices, radios and hundreds of other products manufactured and assembled by Asian slave industries could be obtained at little cost to these retailers.

Thousands of small and medium size American manufacturing industries making these products and other everyday household goods and products, and automotive replacement parts were forced out of business unable to compete with slave workers in Asia. And millions more lost their jobs and were forced into the welfare and unemployment lines. And many millions more Americans lost their homes while corporate profits rose to all time levels.

Foreign countries the world over were eager to take American owned industries into their countries. Many of these foreign industries were being financed by American corporations initially. Others were funded with American foreign aid siphoned off by the wealthy in those countries. Working with self described conservatives, Washington liberals and socialists had eliminated import tariffs on foreign made goods and reduced or eliminated corporate taxes on American corporations doing business in foreign countries. In return they shared the increased profits in the form of election contributions.

At the same time Washington was financing and reducing taxes on goods made in their countries, those foreign countries were imposing huge tariffs on American goods coming into their countries. But it wouldn't have mattered because foreign workers paid at slave wages could not afford to buy American products. Foreign made products produced by slaves workers flooded America and the profit from those product sales was returned to the countries where they were made. American corporations doing business overseas, or who established a telephone number or office overseas had their taxes reduced. While at the same time taxes on the American working families were increased to make up for the losses in government revenues.

Soon America saw their towns and cities flooded with not only cheap goods, but unsafe and poisonous goods as well.

Those who were able to buy needed goods were forced to buy the cheap poisonous goods Americas giant retail industries were bringing in from Asia and unloading on the people. But the Washington Socialists propaganda continued to tell the people over the Socialist controlled media that America would have an industrial boom and profit from these world trade movements.

Then the next globalization move was made by the Washington Socialists. It was called the North American Free Trade Agreement (NAFTA). Again one person, Ross Perot a presidential candidate, spoke out against this agreement. He told the people, if NAFTA was adopted America would hear the loudest sucking noise ever heard anywhere in the world. But the controlled socialist media closed his words out. And the socialists power brokers on wall street and in Washington put him out of the political business.

The controlled media bombarded America with government propaganda. Unbelievable as it seems they were able to convince American workers that soon Central America would become a great dumping ground for every conceivable product American workers made. And opposition to the out of country slave trade were silenced.

Within a few years the giants of the American automotive and tooling industries started their exodus into Central America. Factories were constructed in Mexico and Brazil and our automobile manufacturing , tooling, and industrial technologies were shipped to equip those factories and train those workers. Before long American automotive industries were having their products manufactured and assembled in Mexico at wages one could only consider slave wages. And America saw more plant closings across the country. And millions more American workers lost their jobs, cars and homes. And the unemployment and welfare lines grew across America.

But the socialist controlled media continued to support these globalization policies. They supported Washington's policies and kept silent about the destruction facing American workers as the result of Washington's adoption of United Nations policies. The industrialists and their Washington counterparts, union haters one and all, continued to use every policy possible to destroy the American industrial and manufacturing capabilities. Yet with welfare payments and other giveaways the socialists convinced the union leaders and the workers to support the liberal candidates and their policies, believing it would bring them new jobs and industrial growth.

The betrayal of the American workers by the Washington socialists was one of the greatest betrayals of a nation of people of all times. But that betrayal was never reported by the socialist controlled media. And the people were now so mired in debts and starvation they no longer had the strength to resist. Then the

Washington Socialists, urged on by American industries and the New World Order leaders made their next globalization move. That move was called the Central American Free Trade Agreement (CAFTA).

The CAFTA agreement allowed American industries to move deeper into Central America. Soon clothing industries, textile industries, computer technologies, automotive parts suppliers and dozens of smaller industries began to relocate deeper into Central America for even cheaper wages. Again thousands of small American industries were forced to close, unable to compete with cheap low cost slave labor. Millions more of American workers found themselves displaced and standing in welfare and unemployment lines. And many more lost their homes and were forced into the alleys and shadows of society, living in third world conditions. The alleys and sidewalks were now beginning to look like third world countries, with whole families living amidst the garbage and trash strewn about the streets and sidewalks.

To compound the situation, and eliminate all hope for the American working families, Washington continued the wholesale destruction of the remains of what was once the American Labor Movement. Fulfilling Washington's allegiance with United Nations treaties they opened our borders to migrants, immigration policies were ignored and our borders were kept open for all who chose to cross over. An invasion of illegal immigrants across our southern borders was encouraged by the granting of amnesty to twenty million of these criminal invaders. Washington didn't seem to care that many were bringing in their truckloads of illegal drugs and spreading out across the country marketing their poisonous drugs.

The issuance of driving licenses and voter registration rights to these criminal immigrants became an easy way for liberal socialist legislators to remain in office. Free educations, free medical care, and housing subsidies provided for their offspring encouraged millions more to cross our unguarded borders. No one knows how many millions of non citizen votes were cast and counted in national and local elections to insure the election and re-election of Liberals and Socialists dedicated to turning America over to the Communists and Socialists running the United Nations. The invasion and employment of illegal immigrants in jobs not yet transferred to Asia or Central America reduced the wage levels for all jobs remaining in America. Wages were now on a level equal to third world countries while the cost of homes, automobiles and clothing remained at the high pre-globalization prices.

Civil strife was becoming commonplace as African Americans and poor whites clashed with illegal immigrants fighting over part time work that paid what one could only call slave wages. Small American industries that had not yet been forced out of business had no choice but to employ workers at wages comparable to Asian and Central American wages if they were to remain alive. American workers were forced to compete with illegal immigrants for jobs paying part time slave wages in the service industries, hotels, motels, Inns, restaurants and janitorial services.

Illegal immigrants were also taking over the jobs in the building trades. Former American workers who erected the buildings, lay the bricks and blocks, dry walled their interiors, painted, installed roofing and windows were now forced to compete with these illegal workers for these former good paying jobs that now paid slave wages. And millions more found themselves standing in the welfare and unemployment lines, and millions more lost their homes and were forced to exist in the alleys and shadows in third world conditions.

Meanwhile, on wall street, members of the Council on Foreign Relations and their counterparts in Washington and leaders of the United Nations continued their policies aimed at the destruction of what was once the American Dream. And the controlled press and media was silent. Import taxes were placed on all American made products shipped offshore while abolishing tariffs on goods and products manufactured overseas and imported into America. Budget deficits continued to climb and working class citizens saw more and more taxes taken from their reduced earnings to make up the deficits, and had less and less to live on.

One segment of the American industrial base still remained thus far untouched. But the Washington Socialists were ready to address that issue which was of concern to the UN. First they built a twelve lane super highway stretching from Mexico City thru America ending in Canada. Customs and immigration policies were ignored by Washington for all who entered America from Canada or Mexico. Millions of Arabic Mid-East citizens crossed over the borders from Canada into America. Taking over the motel, hotel and restaurant chains across the country. American workers now found themselves competing with Mideast refugees as well as Latinos for these low pay service jobs.

Then came the policy aimed at destroying the last vestige of American labor. The American trucking industries. The southern borders were opened up for Mexican and other Central American countries. Newly formed trucking companies, owned by international investors, were given a free pass to start transporting goods, manufactured in Central American countries and Mexico, into and across America to nationwide retail outlets. Thousands of American independent truckers saw their life savings, invested in trucks and trailers, lost within weeks as they were replaced by foreign owned transportation companies. And the lack of customs inspections gave a free pass to all who came bringing in their dangerous cargos of illegal drugs and criminal immigrants.

Finally teamsters union leaders started to complain about the loss of jobs, and more important to them, the reduced numbers of union dues caused by the loss of thousands of American trucking jobs. But their voices were raised to late to stop the carnage on American highways and the loss of American jobs. And the jobs losses in the transportation industries were just beginning. Before long, goods and products manufactured in Asia arriving at our seaports were being unloaded by Mexican slave workers or starving American workers then distributed across America by the Central American, primarily Mexican, trucking companies. American air cargo workers who unloaded, sorted and reloaded air freight soon found themselves competing with illegal criminal immigrants for jobs unloading air freight and reloading the freight onto trucks operated by Mexican companies. Jobs that now paid slave wages due to the numbers of illegal immigrants and unemployed workers forced to work for slave wages.

Aged and poorly equipped trucks, which no American trucker would have been permitted to operate, were operated primarily by Mexican citizens who were not required to have insurance or operators licenses when operating in America. These drivers, unable to read English and operating unsafe equipment, were involved in hundreds of accidents costing thousands of lives and untold damages.

These Drivers were paid slave wages only a fraction of the wages of former American transportation operators. Yes former, because American trucking companies and independent owner operators were forced out of business, unable to compete with slave industries. Former small business operators were forced to close unable to compete with foreign owned businesses managed and operated with low cost immigrant workers. And thousands more American workers lost their jobs and joined the lines at unemployment and welfare agencies.

The unemployment numbers in America rose to more than twenty percent, but those numbers were misleading. Those Americans who had jobs were working in part time positions at slave wages. Government had long ago abolished bankruptcy laws and replaced them with debtor prisons. Those condemned to such warehouses were treated the same as imprisoned criminals. Globalization had worked. America was fast becoming a third world country. The collapse of America was approaching, but the people were hopelessly mired in apathy and fear of government.

When new automobile sales plummeted American automobile production companies suddenly were faced with the fact that low paid American workers could not afford the price of their products. Nor could the foreign workers afford automobiles on their dollar a day wages. American carmakers turned to their globalization partners for assistance. American producers were forced to merge with or outright sell their corporations to foreign interests. Some were closed altogether unable to sell their slave produced products. Globalization had worked but not in the way American workers had been told it would. Nor did it happen the way corporate giants thought it would. Giant corporations who had believed the cheap foreign labor would double their profits soon found the huge profits they had realized initially were disappearing.

Then something happened the wealthy industrialists had not taken into account. The banking and mortgage companies fell into financial disarray. They were now faced with the foreclosures on tens of millions of automobiles and millions of homes previously owned by employed American workers. Many of these homes had been overpriced and sold with adjustable interest rates so those in the building industries, realtors, banks and mortgage corporations could reap a generous profit.

Now with tens of millions of abandoned homes and foreclosures at an all time high, realtors and investment firms and bank and mortgage company failures were rising.

The banking industries now were asking an indebted government to tax American workers to bail them out. But with tax revenues at an all time low, due to business failures and low paid American workers, government was hard pressed to assist their former partners of globalization policies. The international financiers and investors once eager to give the American government credit had turned away for more reliable investments overseas. The printing presses were shut down, no more currency was being printed because no one would risk backing a failing government. Failing banking and mortgage corporations turned to foreign investors trying to salvage their corporations.

But foreign investors were now unwilling to risk investing in America. The dollar was steadily losing value in the world markets and the American dollar was now worth half it's value. The American stock exchanges, wall street and others, saw half the value of their stocks and bonds disappear. Many countries formerly eager to grab the American dollar now were turning to other currencies, such as the Euro dollar or the Chinese yen. The value of American currency, once the most valued currency in the history of the world, was officially devalued on the world markets. America was financially bankrupt and unable to repay the national debt owed to foreign investors.

At the urging of The United Nations, directors of the International Monetary Fund (IMF) declared the United States to be an indebted nation incapable of repaying the federal debt. America was declared to be a poor credit risk. The value of the American dollar fell even more and high international interest rates were imposed against the United States. In order to print money to pay government expenses, the United States Federal reserve bank had to pay increasingly high interest rates on government bonds and securities purchased by foreign investors, when they could find someone willing to take the risk of losing their investment. And the American national debt continued to rise.

Those high interest rates were then passed on to American banks and eventually to the American people in the form of higher taxes. But even then most investors turned away from American bonds and securities because the probability of losing their investments, should America face an economic and financial collapse. Which was becoming a real probability.

Without adequate credit to finance the printing of money our government was forced to stop issuing loans to American banks or do so at an interest rate none could afford to pay. Corporate stock for remaining American owned industries was falling to lows comparable to the great depression levels. Modern day carpet baggers, mostly foreign nationals, were moving into every corner of America. They commenced to grab control of our airports, shipyards, automobile industries, air cargo transporters and agricultural lands where they could profit from low wage workers, immigrants and nationals, who now made up the American work force of former American owned industries.

Next the agriculture communities began to feel the effects of globalization. The inability of American families to buy high priced food supplies had caused a reduction in the prices farmers could get for their products. Foreign markets that had always depended upon American aid in the form of free food supplies found America could no longer supply their needs. Foreign buyers now could only offer reduced prices for agricultural products. Small family farms, unable to pay their mortgages, were facing foreclosure. Even large corporate agricultural producers were facing bankruptcy. America became a nation of starving people.

Globalization was sold to America and American workers as the next great industrial revolution. It was promised that tens of millions of jobs would come to America once foreigners could afford to purchase goods made in America. And to be sure some jobs were created in America. But these were jobs limited to service industries where American workers had to compete with illegal immigrants. And these were jobs in slave industries where workers slaved long hours in unsafe conditions for slave wages.

Those few American industries that remained were now owned and operated by foreign investors from Japan, Germany, and other foreign countries.

They came to take advantage of the millions of unemployed and displaced former American workers. Workers who had no choice but to work, wherever they could find it, at whatever wages offered, or see their families face starvation The people should have remembered that the definition of revolution is Upheaval. During the planned Washington globalization movement four million good paying jobs went to Asia, another two million jobs went to Central America, while national upheaval came to America.

With sufficient taxable income no longer available due to the millions of American workers now idle many government services and programs began their collapse. The public school system deteriorated until there was none. The cost of housing, feeding, educating and providing medical care to fifty million criminal immigrants added trillions to the federal and state budgets. With government unable to meet the cost of welfare immigrants turned to a life of criminal activity more destructive than ever before.

The number of unemployed and underemployed workers now exceeded the number of employed workers in America. Tax collections had fallen to an all time low. Because of unemployment and low wages few American families had income for government to seize. So the schools were closed and replaced with government operated indoctrination centers. There they were fed and clothed and indoctrinated into becoming government enforcers.

Medical emergency treatment centers and many hospitals were also forced to close their doors. The closing of manufacturing plants and other industries had led to the termination of company sponsored medical insurance plans and American citizens could not afford family medical expenses on their own, so the sick and the aged were untreated and forgotten. Medical practitioners had for the most part been forced out of business also. Those that remained were caring for their patients in exchange for food or anything of useable value.

Disease and pestilence were everywhere. Small pox, Tuberculosis and Aids were now at epidemic proportions and nearing pandemic numbers. Many of these diseases had been eliminated from the American scene years before.

But fifty million illegal, unchecked and untested immigrants had brought the scourge of infectious diseases back to America. Pharmaceutical manufacturers had moved to Asia to lower their costs and were not inclined to ship their products back to a land where the people and the government could not afford their drugs.

America was nearing economic collapse. For more than fifty years American workers had been taxed so Washington could give those billions of dollars to foreign countries around the world in foreign aid giveaways. But not one of those countries offered assistance of any kind to the American people now that they were in need. The trillions of dollars in foreign aid had not bought Washington the loyalty of one country. There was no United

Nations call for countries to provide medical and food supplies to the starving people of America.

Globalization had come to America. But it was not the great industrial revolution promised. There was no rush to America for American made goods and products, because there were no goods or products being made in America. The great American industrial and economic might had been dismantled and the prosperity of American workers was lost in the process.

The great industrial boom had gone to China, India, Japan, Europe and Central America. China was now the fastest growing industrial country in the world. Other Asian and Central American countries were prospering and growing as well. The only growth taking place in America was the expanding ownership of banks, mortgage companies, hotels, Inns, and restaurants by newly arrived Arabic and Asian investors.

Globalization had wrought National upheaval in the form of unemployment, disease and pestilence. The socialists membership of the Council on Foreign Relations had won. Malaise had settled on America. America was no longer capable of influencing world events. The American people had neither the will nor the courage to prevent the New World Order, and their Socialists partners in Washington, from taking the last steps necessary to hasten the collapse of America. The steps to collapse are limited, and we are approaching that last step.

If there is any doubt in your mind as to whether the final outcome of globalization policies could turn out as I have predicted in this chapter, then consider the following examples of Washington policies. Policies just taken during March of 2008. I believe these two actions taken by our leaders show better than anything else, exactly where the Washington socialists real loyalties lie.

First: During March 2008, the Defense Department, with the blessings of the congress and the President, awarded a thirty billion dollar aircraft production contract to a foreign owned company. When bids were first requested for the contract, an American aircraft company, bowing aircraft, came in with the lowest bid. Then due to congressional pressures, specifications for the contract were revised and the contract was then awarded to a foreign company owned by a French Consortium.

One can only imagine what was offered the congressional member for his efforts and success in getting the contract awarded to the foreign owned company. And what was offered members of the defense department, white house and other members of congress who raised no objections to this raw deal for Americans. I'm forced to question where their loyalties lie, and clearly this indicated they are not with America.

Secondly: If you still believe Washington or the wall street socialists, have the interest of the American citizens at heart consider this. In March 2008, the Federal Reserve Banking leaders, acting upon the call of Congress decided the following action. They decided to loan two hundred billion dollars (that's 200 Billion Dollars) to the banking and mortgage corporations who had fleeced then foreclosed on American homeowners, after overpricing their homes, raising their interest rates and forcing them into bankruptcy.

Wouldn't it seem more fitting, and more American, for the government, and their bankers, to have helped the millions of unemployed American workers forced into foreclosure by greedy banks and mortgage companies, than to help those who profited from the peoples foreclosures? Again, where does this indicate the loyalties of Washington and wall street lie? Certainly they do not appear to lie with the American people or America.

Consider this. In the year 2007 the three major oil producing companies reaped a world breaking record profit in the hundreds of billion of dollars. At the same time they were receiving taxpayer subsidies and government tax reductions. The giant retailer Wal-Mart, once founded and succeeding on made in America products, reaped tens of billions in profits from their cheap Chinese made goods, and billions more from the low cost American labor now used to sell their products. Wouldn't it be more American to have shown loyalty to the American workers by lowering their taxes, than to increase our working families taxes while adding to the profits of these corporations?

Sadly, the people are primarily responsible for the direction Washington is taking America. It is the people who have voted the socialist in power and the people who vote to keep them there. Will things change? Will the people learn? It certainly does not appear they have or will in the near future. Consider; As election 2008 approaches the people have decided on three presidential candidates, one of which will be in control for the next four years. And that is time enough to complete the destruction of America.

One candidate is an avowed liberal, whom many would consider to be a socialist. Her programs of education, medical care, welfare, military preparedness, foreign policies and national defense of America can only be described as socialists policies. Another is a person who was born of Moslem ancestry, schooled in Moslem schools, attends a church whose minister speaks hatred for America and all white people. Certainly enough reason to wonder who he is , where his beliefs lie. His programs for education, medical care, welfare, foreign policies and national defense of America can only be described as socialists policies.

A third candidate is a former military officer who was captured and held captive for many years by the enemy in Viet Nam. None can question his spirit and strength in overcoming that tragic period in his life. But many question his support for such socialist programs as limiting the free speech of citizens by the McCain Feingold law he sponsored.

All three candidates support the continuing criminal invasion coming across our borders by their support for programs of amnesty, welfare, free educations, free medical care, subsidized housing and all the other freebies the invaders receive. Support for such programs do nothing but encourage the invasion to continue. All three candidates support the United Nations GATT treaty and the NAFTA and CAFTA treaties, despite the fact those treaties have cost America five million good paying jobs.

Sadly, Americans have already made their choice to elect a socialist candidate to become the president. Because a vote for any of the above candidates is a vote for a continuation of the policies of socialism. It is a vote for continuation of the GATT, NAFTA and CAFTA treaties, and all the Globalization policies that destroyed the Industrial and manufacturing capacity of America. Globalization policies they were told would bring a new industrial revolution to America.

Alas, The people should have remembered the definition of revolution is upheaval, because the industrial revolution promised American workers came in the form of upheaval. The socialists have succeeded. The industrial base of America has been destroyed. One more step towards national collapse is complete.

Abolishing Our Constitution

The next destructive policy instituted by Washington and Socialist the world over was and had always been their ultimate goal. This time their efforts were directed towards eliminating American national sovereignty and our constitutional system of government and laws. The Socialists and Communists leading the United Nations were making rapid progress in reducing the financial, industrial, and military power of America. They now began to use all their power over the socialists in Washington to dismantle the authorities inherent in the constitutional processes of America.

To date the United Nations has adopted more than five hundred multinational treaties, agreements, which are legally binding upon member states that ratify them. Washington agreed with and ratified many of those treaties. Among the United Nations most pervasive actions has been to convince member states that a body of international law must be developed and enforced worldwide. All member states would have to eventually abolish their national sovereignty and constitutions and bring their judicial systems in compliance with United Nations international laws. Those that refused to do so would be sanctioned by the United Nations.

One must seriously question whether any of our presidents or those in congress have ever read, let alone studied the United Nations charter they ratified. One must also question whether our presidents or those in congress have ever read or studied the more than five hundred multi national agreements the leaders of the United Nations have adopted. Many of those treaties ratified by Washington.

If any have then we have to question their loyalties to our constitution and our country. Why would they join and remain a strong supporter of a communist and socialist controlled organization known as the United Nations. Our founders warned us about becoming involved in treaties with foreign states, but our leaders have ignored their warnings. We have been betrayed. All America should rise and demand we get out of the United Nations and throw them out of our country.

The United Nations is a totalitarian organization. The Socialists and Communist leaders of that organization are dedicated anti-American rulers and world dominion is their goal. Consider these United Nations agreements if you are in doubt as to their intentions.

In 1992 The United States president and congress agreed to the United Nations Agenda For Peace which states; The time for Absolute Sovereignty and National Constitutions for individual states has passed. Washington agreed with that agenda. To insure that the UN carries out it's goal of world control it is using United States military forces and economic power to impose it's will upon the world.

Article 47 of the United Nations Charter establishes a Military staff committee which has been given Command and Control of all forces serving the United Nations. Washington agreed to this article, thus we now see our military forces wearing United Nations uniforms and commanded by UN commanders.

United Nations leaders have coordinated and controlled the use of American military forces and American taxpayers money with the purpose of decimating our financial and military resources. Since the year 1950 more than 100 thousand of our military forces have lost their lives and hundreds of thousands more have been disabled fighting in UN sponsored wars. These have all been, by design, no win wars, commencing with Korea. To insure we lost their wars, borders were established in most of those conflicts that prohibited our forces from pursuing the enemy beyond a certain point.

Not one of the countries we went to war to help were any better off afterwards than they were before those wars started. In every instance after we fled or withdrew, we rebuilt those countries. Then control of those countries fell under the control of Communist or Socialist dictators. Every war we have been in since World War Two was a war the United Nations wanted us to wage. Why do we get into these wars? Because Washington agreed with United Nations Article 47, giving our military forces over to the United Nations control whenever they tell us to.

I ask you, show me anyplace in our constitution where it gives the president the authority to send our forces into so called peace fighting missions, upon the orders of, or under the command and control of foreign rulers. Our constitution clearly reserves the power to declare war only to the congress. But the members of congress have avoided their responsibilities by permitting the presidents to send our forces into war for the United Nations, by classifying these wars as conflicts, that do not require a congressional declaration of war. All the congress has to do is supply the money to wage these so called conflicts.

I would remind the readers that Article 5 of our constitution provides only one procedure for amending our constitution. That is by a vote of the people of all states with a three fourths majority of the states ratifying the proposed amendment. However, on 26 September 1961, the congress of these United States adopted public law 87297, The Arms Control and Disarmament Act. That law legalizes the transfer of United States military Forces into the United Nations military force, and places them under the control of the United Nations Security Council. This action agreed to by the presidents and congress is a violation of our constitution. I believe our presidents and legislators should be held accountable for their traitorous actions.

The authority to commit Americans into war has been transferred from the Congress of these United States to the

Security Council of the United Nations. While this was taking place America was also arbitrarily deprived of a veto vote in the Security Council. Thereafter making Washington submit to all United Nations actions without a veto voice in final decisions. Washington's agreeing to this is a deceitful and criminal betrayal of all Americans by our presidents and the Congress who swear an oath to protect, preserve, and defend our constitution.

I would remind you, when a soldier fails to uphold his oath of enlistment, no matter how fearful the conditions are on the battlefield, He is charged with desertion and faces a sentence of death or imprisonment. I ask you, why then should not a president or a member of the congress, who intentionally and voluntarily violate their oath to defend, protect and preserve our constitution be required to face charges of treason and be tried as traitors?

Among the United Nations most pervasive actions is actions to convince member states that a body of international law must be established. All member states would then have to abolish their national sovereignty and their national constitutions. Once completed all nations, including the United States, would have to bring their judicial systems in compliance with United Nations International criminal and civil laws. These actions have been ongoing for several years and are now urgent policies of reform for the communist and totalitarian leaders in the United Nations.

Washington has given the United Nations control of our military and financial resources, which were then used for the primary purpose of reducing Americas capacity to resist the final takeover of America by the United Nations. They have succeeded. Thirty years and more than a dozen no win United Nations ordered wars decimated our military forces. And these conflicts have added trillions to our national debt. Our military forces have been scattered in more than one hundred countries around the world, mostly at the request of those who rule the United Nations.

Another pervasive action initiated by the UN, and directed at the United States, was the adoption of a multilateral treaty at the 1990 United Nations convention in New York. A treaty Washington ratified. That treaty establishes the principle of equal treatment with nationals, for all migrants who enter a country, regardless of the legal status of the migrant workers. That treaty creates standards concerning migrant workers to which we must adhere. It combined six international human rights treaties then in effect, and establishes an international body to review how well countries are complying with it's provisions. So Remember, the United Nations are watching to see how criminals crossing our borders are treated.

That 1990 convention, of which the US was in agreement, creates different categories of migrants which was internationally agreed on. That treaty also requires that the governments, of countries that are invaded by migrants, initiate protective actions on behalf of migrant workers. At the time the American people were disagreeing with amnesty programs and federal handouts to illegal migrants, the congress refused to secure our borders and expel illegal criminals crossing our borders.

They apparently did so because International treaties required Americas borders to remain open to refugees and migrants. The United Nations leaders believe that treaty gave the international courts the power to overturn our courts convictions of illegal migrant robbers, rapists and murderers.

Neither the Congress or the president objected to the international courts claim of jurisdiction in the cases of illegal immigrants. In fact, the president appeared to have more concern about hurting the international courts feelings, or being accused of failing to enforce United Nations laws upon American citizens, than he had for the American citizens who were raped and murdered. President Bush appears to agree with the Federal Courts decision that illegal migrants who commit crimes against American citizens should be turned over to their consulates rather than have them face charges in our courts. Why else would He allow our border guards to remain in prison while the criminals they stopped from smuggling illegal drugs into our country are released and given a free pass to smuggle more drugs across our border?

These illegal, criminal, immigrants have been given a free pass into America where they obtain free educations, medical care, food and lodging. They have reduced the wage scale for jobs in America and their presence has forced American workers to compete with them for low wage jobs. Untold thousands of Americans have seen their auto insurance rates rise to pay the cost of damages caused by uninsured unlicensed immigrant drivers. And American workers find their taxes increased to pay the cost of welfare and rising crime committed by illegal immigrants.

Another dangerous betrayal of American citizens and decimation of our constitution is without doubt unknown to our people. In Article 1, Section 8, paragraph 17: Our constitution states very clearly, only the Congress has jurisdiction and exclusive legislation regarding any Federal land or buildings purchased from and by the consent of a state. Yet in violation of our constitutional law and using presidential Directives and Executive orders, State lands belonging to the sovereign people of America have been repeatedly seized by the central government and placed under the control of the United Nations.

Consider these facts. In 1998, as if Congressional greed and stupidity wasn't enough, America took part in a master plan known as, United Nations Agenda 21. That conference was a follow up to the 1992 United Nations Earth Summit. Several treaties were adopted, each designed to destroy our national sovereignty.

One such treaty is the Bio-diversity treaty which calls for global regions to be designated and placed under the control of Non Governmental Organizations (NGOs), which is a code word for organizations under United Nations control. Since 1978, without State approval or public hearings, and without the knowledge or consent of the American people, forty seven United Nations Biospheres have been established in America consisting of more than 43 million acres (68,000) sq. miles of United States Land.

Two designations of "International Status" The UNESCO Reserves and the World Heritage Sites were done without Congressional approval or public hearings. Our presidents, and the Congress have conspired to give the United Nations Bureaucrats the final oversight of these sites thru their United Nations Non Governmental Organizations, NGO's) , and no public hearings, or approval of the people in the United States were obtained. And they did so in violation of our constitution.

Biosphere land reserves in the United States, controlled by the United Nations as of 1998, contained a land mass larger than the state of Colorado. The United States now has 20 World Heritage sites, 18 of which are national parks and preserves.

Sixty eight percent (68%) of our national parks and reserves are designated as United Nations World Heritage Sites or Biosphere Reserves or both. Were you aware the statue of liberty and Independence hall are among the sites under the control of the United Nations. Can you imagine the founders of our country and our constitution selling out the people in such a way?

We are in this mess because the Congress and our Presidents have ignored and violated two provisions of our Constitution. The first, Article 1V, Section Eight, Clause Seventeen of the Constitution, limits Federal ownership of land to only those few acres surrounding the capital buildings. The Second, Article 1V, Section 3, Clause 2, Specifically designates Congress as the overseer of all US property and more importantly; forbids federal, or any takeover, of state land.

Again I say, we have been betrayed by the Washington Socialists and the Council on Foreign Relations whose members organized the United Nations.

The Socialistic leaders of the United Nations no doubt believe that since they were given control over considerable areas of land in America that this also gives them jurisdiction over matters such as immigration and our courts. Or perhaps they believed that since Washington gave them control of our land, they would give them control of our courts. In view of the actions and decisions by the congress and our presidents it would appear they were right on both counts.

President Clinton took an oath to defend our constitution against all enemies. Yet He was so in favor of the United Nations and it's Bio-diversity programs that He called upon the United Nations to support his decision to ban a gold mine near Yellowstone national Park. His decision to steal 1.7 million acres of Utah land and place it into a Grand Staircase-Escalante national monument, under the control of the United Nations NGO organization could only have been based upon his support for United Nations goals for American land use.

Our Constitution has never been amended to allow federal ownership of any land, other than those parcels in and near the capital originally authorized by our founding fathers. And our constitution prohibits foreign powers from assuming control over any American soil under any circumstances. Yet we have surrendered sovereign rights to 75 million acres of the most beautiful parts of America to the United Nations. America has been betrayed. The people have been betrayed.

By giving the United Nations control of our military forces, ownership of our state lands, and instituting United Nations policies regarding welfare and immigration, the Congress and our presidents went full ahead with the abolishment of our Sovereignty as a nation and the destruction of our Constitution. Today our military force is a shambles, our manufacturing capacity has been destroyed and as a nation we are 10 trillion dollars in debt and insolvent.

Because of the high taxes levied upon and seized from working families American citizens are now an indebted people. I wonder how many Americans are aware of this sell out of America. Did anyone hear the liberal controlled media discuss it? No, and you won't hear them talk about it. It's wake up time but that may be too late. Read, and teach your children to read. Watch and teach them to watch something besides the nakedness and filth coming over the media airwaves and the movie theaters.

Isn't it odd that while many American citizens and some foreign states disagree with our current excursion into Iraq, we have not heard one word of disagreement coming from the leaders of the United Nations. Of course we have not and will not hear any complaints from the United Nations leaders, or their Socialist partners around the world. After all, the Iraq war is taking us ever closer to financial and military collapse as a nation which plays us into the hands of the communist leaders of the United Nations. That is why on 20 December 2007, the United Nations issued a resolution advising Washington to remain in Iraq.

American trade and tariff policies have been based upon United Nations agreements for two decades. American national defense policies have been based upon United Nations agreements for fifty years. Our public education policies have been revised and regulated to suit the atheist and socialists for three decades. The Socialization of America has left our country without an industrial base, with a decimated military and ten trillion dollars in debt.

With the American economy destroyed, the people demoralized and government left in the hands of socialists it becomes only a matter of when, not if, America Sovereignty as a nation will end. Apathy and malaise have consumed the people. America is fast approaching the last steps towards national collapse. America watched while socialism took us one step closer to national collapse. Time is running out for America, and the clock is clicking.

Destroy The Christian Base

There are two parts to this chapter. Part one is a summary of policies and actions taken or concurred with by our government and others and the effect they have had on the Christian faith of our fathers. Part two is a fictionalAccount of what I believe those of the Christian faith may face in the future America..

PART 1.
Where American Christianity is today.

The New World Order, and their Socialists supporters in America and from around the world, are determined to erase Christianity from the face of America. A step they feel necessary if America is to collapse. For several decades The faith of our fathers, our firm belief in Christ our Savior, has been under attack from within America and from without. Those dedicated to destroying America understand that the strength and resolve of the American people comes from our faith in Christ. Those who would destroy us are well aware that before we can be enslaved the Christian faith of our fathers must be erased, or driven underground, from the face of America.

When the Socialist membership of the Council on Foreign Relations and their Washington partners, consorted with the Soviet and Chinese Communists to establish the United Nations, they were content to allow the United States military power destroy the Axis regime of Adolf Hitler and his partners in Japan. The leaders of these organizations were well aware the historical records of those nations would someday bring them into the fold of the United Nations membership. But they wanted them to come in as defeated nations without the power to threaten the future of the United Nations.

For several decades the Socialist concentrated on weakening the financial and military resources of America by keeping America involved in wars and conflicts. At the same time multilateral treaties were adopted by the United Nations that slowly reduced the effect of the Christian heritage in Washington politics. Treaties that required member states, including America, to accept immigrants from countries around the world, many of which were from anti-Christian countries.

Because of United Nations immigration policies the people who were the Christian Majority in America are no longer a majority with numbers sufficient to influence governmental policies. While the United Nations leaders were working towards their goal of reducing the effect of Christian believers in Washington, other Socialist and Atheistic organizations inside America were pursuing various legal means to overturn two centuries of laws based in part upon our constitutional founders strong belief in God.

The American Civil Liberties Union, a consortium of atheist, filed hundreds of lawsuits against federal, state and local governments and schools claiming violation of the separation of church and state provisions of the Constitution. County schools were taken to court for exhibiting religious displays, such as the ten commandments, on school properties. Lawsuits were filed to prohibit and prevent any discussion of religion in the schools. Even our courthouses were forced to remove In God We Trust from over their doors. Christianity became last on the Washington agenda of principles to preserve.

Federal and State judicial appointees made by liberal presidents and socialist congressional leaders seem more than eager to side with the American Civil Liberties Union in such lawsuits. This resulted in it becoming a violation of federal and state laws to display or discuss the principles of Christianity in our schools or anyplace upon federal, state, or government owned or operated properties. Even in the public workplace no references to God were permitted. The socialist controlled media joined right in and we no longer hear broadcasters saying Merry Christmas over the air waves. Only the expression of happy holidays is heard.

Over a span of three decades school students were exposed to a continuous barrage of evolutionary teachings. Students were contained in schools for twelve years, eight hours each day, being taught their ancestors crawled out of swamps. They were taught that their ancestors then grew tails and learned to swing in trees and eventually evolved to the point where they learned to stand and walk upright. Somehow they even learned to talk and became capable of speaking in the various languages of the world. (I guess they are taught not to ask why nothing is crawling out of the swamps and evolving anymore)

After years of indoctrination in such theories, from the time they were five years of age until completing school at the ages of seventeen and eighteen years, many children came to believe these theories of evolution. Then as some went on to receive the socialist teachings in college their introduction into the world of atheism continued. Judicial appointees installed by Washington socialists and atheist prohibited any discussion of our Christian faith in the public schools. Many so taught questioned the faith of their parents, asking for proof that their school taught theories were not accurate. Parents who were limited to a few moments each morning and a few hours each evening with their children were hard pressed to overcome eight hours a day for fourteen years of forced school indoctrination into the world of atheism.

After several generations of forced evolutionary indoctrination, with exposure to the teachings of Christianity restricted to a few hours at home and church, children drifted away from the beliefs of their parents. Family bonds became a thing of the past in many instances. Many elder citizens find themselves alone with no real relationships with their adult children. Children and young adults who prefer to use mind altering drugs and watch the violence, filth and nakedness on the television and in the theaters have turned their backs on the values of their parents.

After three generations of animalistic indoctrination the behavior of the young took on the characteristics of the animals they were told were their relatives. Males ran from gathering to gathering, from street corner to street corner raping and impregnating their female counterparts. They foraged from neighborhood to neighborhood attacking, robbing, stealing and staking out their territories like the animals have done for centuries. Animals many have come to believe are their ancestors.

The use of illegal drugs became commonplace among the young people and marauding gangs fought for territorial rights to market their drugs. Territories were based mostly on the predominant race of the community thus these gang fights became a conflict between the races in many instances. Crimes of every nature increased until city streets were unsafe for anyone not known in that community.

And while the political elect and the media decried the drugs and violence they used the behaviors of the gangs to pursue the need for gun controls, another primary goal of all socialists in America and the United Nations leaders.

By all accounts this is where we are today. The youth of America have become immune to the teachings and beliefs of our fathers. Our government has encouraged the dissolution of Christian marriages by their legalization of same sex unions. The Christian upbringing of our children in Christian homes has been destroyed with the mandatory teachings of evolution and socialized welfare that encourages animal like behaviors. The practice of, or expression of, our Christian faith in public has been outlawed in most public places, and ridiculed in others.

Government has further encouraged the breakdown of Christian principles by the financing of unchristian behaviors. By rewarding those who have children out of wedlock with welfare payments and subsidies of every nature at the expense of taxpayers.

They further reward those who behave in unchristian criminal behaviors with a lavish lifestyle in prison rather than compelling them to work to pay the cost of their room and board.

The atheistic movie and television producers in Hollywood flood the country with their pornographic materials and proudly display their lifestyle in movies such as, knocked up. Those who reach fame in Hollywood proudly display their children, born out of wedlock, for all the young children of America to see. They proudly display the gay and lesbian lifestyles for the young to see. What an inspirational method of teaching our young this has become. And government leaders seem to find no fault in their doing so.

In part our very own Christian Church leaders must share the blame for the decline of Christianity in America. Organized Christian churches are prohibited from entering into the political scene in America because, they have been Unwilling to give up their tax free status to do so. As the result the voice of organized Christianity is silent, left only to individual Christians to try to elect Christian candidates to public office.

Other policies that encouraged the illegal immigration of non-believers has reduced the influence the Christian community has on American politics. When our country does happen to elect a so called conservative and tries to appoint a constitutional scholar to the bench they are denied appointment by the atheist and socialists in Washington, and in many cases even a hearing, to be considered for appointment to a judicial position.

The erosion and sometimes prohibition of expression of the Christian faith by liberal appointees to the bench has destroyed much of the free expression of our Christian heritage. This is where we are today, but Americans of the Christian faith will face even more severe tests of their individual beliefs in the very near future.

PART TWO.
THE OUTLOOK FOR THE FUTURE OF AMERICAN CHRISTIANITY.

The United Nations leaders will continue their march towards world dominion strengthening their influence over Washington policies. Globalization of trade and tariff policies, and decimation of the American military and industrial might had left America in turmoil. Immigration policies, or lack thereof, had changed the character of America. Christians of European ancestries were now a minority in America, far out numbered by Asian, Arabic, Latinos, and African American citizens. The influence of the Christian is no longer a significant voice in Washington.

Racial and religious strife are rampant between the various religious sects. Gangs of murderous Latino and African American drug dealers and Christian hating Moslem immigrants roamed the streets fighting over their territories. Many of these immigrants had came from countries where the only law was the law of the strongest and most powerful. State and local Law enforcement officers were incapable of stopping the carnage, for they had long been used solely as revenue producers, not crime fighters. And the violence gave the socialist in Washington a cause to support their cries for disarmament of all citizens.

Many Christian families were forced to move out of their homes and into the rural areas for safety. But the gangs, drugs and pillaging followed them wherever they went. Homes were broken into and the older citizens robbed, beaten and murdered in many unprotected rural locations. Christian churches became fair game for thieves and vandals and were becoming a thing of the past. Christian families and friends had been driven underground, so they met in their homes in private to practice their Christian faith. Much like they have been forced to do in other parts of the world.

There was no protection for the Christian family for government no longer felt the votes of this minority was of any consequence to their political goals. The media decried the violence and lack of government actions to end the strife. They kept up a continuous demand for the government to prohibit all private ownership of firearms as a way to end the violence. International Socialist groups and United Nations leaders increased their pressure for America to join the world wide ban on all privately owned firearms.

In Washington the Liberals and Socialists had been waiting for just the right circumstances to make their move to disarm the American people. The public schools indoctrination of three generations into evolutionary atheistic beliefs had all but ended public practices of Christianity in America. America had become a divided country. For more than a century Americans had grown up hunting together as families for food and recreation. But time and public indoctrination had changed the face of America. Hunting was an activity of only a few and Christianity was now confined to the home in the hearts of those who still believed.

Today as the Christmas season approaches we don't hear the media saying merry Christmas. The retail outlets stock their stores with foreign made gifts and toys of every kind and description, with large signs saying, happy holidays, not Merry Christmas. Many of the state capitals no longer put up and decorate Christmas trees, others did so with a sign saying happy holidays in front of them. Some took them down after decorating them, to appease the non believers.

Gone are the movies of our childhood. Clean decent movies that told the story of families working together to improve their lives. The Charlton Hestons and movies like Moses that taught us Biblical history have long departed from the American scene. Television programs that used to feature stories the family could sit and watch together have been replaced by homosexual talk show hosts, gay couples and sex and violence. We have entered into an era of anti Christian teachings cleverly produced to influence the beliefs and behaviors of the young.

Even our president, George Bush, on the twentieth of December 2008, when addressing the press and visitors at the capital building started to say merry Christmas, hesitated, then said in a subdued voice, he hoped they all enjoy the holidays. His fear of relating the holidays to Christ was so evident, it was commented on by the television announcer.

The practice of Christianity has been driven underground, unable to influence governmental actions or policies. Another step along the road to collapse has been completed. The faith of our fathers, the base that held America together, is no more.

Disarming America

The next step, and perhaps the most dangerous for all America, was the Washington Socialists decision to endorse the United Nations gun control efforts. Will they be successful in their joint efforts to disarm the American people. My seventy eight years of observing the changing attitudes of the people tell me they will succeed. I fear the courage and faith of America has been replaced with apathy, malaise and fear of government.

Part one of this chapter described the actions and policies that government has already instituted to prepare the people for the disarming of America, and the collapse of our nation. Part two of this chapter describes the actions and policies, that I predict, government will institute in the not to distant future to disarm the American people. And this chapter describes what I believe will be a futile attempt, of a few citizens, to stop the governments betrayal of the people.

Part one:

The primary objective of the United Nations Socialist and Communist leaders is to eliminate private ownership of firearms by American citizens. Their objective is supported by Socialist and Communists the world over. And by the membership of the Council on Foreign Relations. Their purpose, to insure that the United States people would not have the capacity to rebel against the dissolution of our national sovereignty, our constitution and our laws. Gun control is the top agenda of the United Nations. Gun laws are currently much freer in America than in the rest of the world. But a web of United Nations treaties, of which Washington is a part, is directed at abolishing our second amendment right to keep and bear firearms.

Documents from the United Nations own web page (http://www.un.org) makes it clear they are very serious about disarming American citizens. On December 22, 1995, the United Nations announced the launch of a study of small arms. That worldwide study was financed by the Japanese government. The Canadian government furnished a number of gun control advocates to assist in that United Nations study. Stewart Allen, chief of the intelligence division of the United States bureau of Alcohol, Tobacco and Firearms also was a member representing the United States.

According to a December 22, 1995 United Nations press release, American police, customs and our military leaders also joined in the survey effort. I am forced to ask whether anyone outside of Washington heard of this United Nations study, or of our involvement in it. Certainly we did not hear our government or the controlled media discuss it. Don't you believe the people are entitled to know about the decisions made, and be given a chance to voice their opinions. Is this what we really want from Washington, a wall of secrecy closing out the unconstitutional actions of those who now control the future of America?

The Japanese convinced the United Nations to approve a resolution authorizing the United Nations Crime Commission to consider various measures to regulate guns. Members of that United Nations Crime Commission spoke of an alarming increase in the proliferation of small arms. They stated their use by drug traffickers and criminal gangs posed a grave threat to public safety and the rule of law. One should note, that same rhetoric was used in the United States by Handgun Control and The Brady Bunch and their Socialist leaders in the congress. Isn't it odd that in every state where the right of people to keep and carry firearms, the incidence of violent crimes committed by gun owners has decreased significantly. And more important, in every country where the people were armed, that country remained a free state. And in every country that was disarmed that nation eventually fell under the control of Socialists, Communists or Nazis. Except for talk radio, these facts were ignored by the American media.

The United Nations secretary general was urged to continue efforts to curb the illicit circulation of small arms, and to collect and confiscate guns in the affected states. Americans should beware. The United Nations convinced the governments of England, Australia and many others to disarm their people, and America is next on their list. Since disarming, those countries have been overrun by crime and in many ways Moslem immigrants. The fact of the matter is, the United Nations General Agreement on Trade and Tariffs (GATT) treaty, of which Washington is a member, gave the United Nations significant authorities over world commerce. The United Nations is increasingly taking more jurisdictional authority in regulating the transportation of firearms, and gun control and gun confiscation in America is high on their agenda.

United Nations international organizations directed at the United States have already started to transfer sovereignty from our national government to unelected national organizations. When the GATT(General Agreement on Trade and Tariffs) Treaty was adopted it was said the treaty would not be inconsistent with United States Laws. But former speaker of the House, Gingrich, described the GATT Treaty as the same as the Maastricht treaty governing most of Europe , which was used to destroy much of the European countries national sovereignty. The fact is, that GATT treaty and others are transferring a significant level of United States sovereignty to United Nations international organizations, just as Gingrich said it would.

With the power granted by their Trade and Tariff treaties (GATT) the United Nations can regulate, or even prevent, the shipping of guns made in foreign countries to the United States. And the Socialists in Washington are eager to have them do so. Already they have, with the support and assistance of United Nations representatives, used Unconstitutional Laws to restrict

US citizens from purchasing guns. They have used Socialists Judicial appointees to levy taxes and fines upon United States gun manufacturing companies to drive them out of business. Once firearms are no longer made in America, the United Nations can prevent any from being shipped into America. And remember this, the guns and ammunition our military personnel use are manufactured overseas.

With American gun manufacturing eliminated, and the shipping of guns from outside stopped by the United Nations, all that would remain to be done to disarm American citizens, would be the to use unconstitutional government laws and government enforcement agencies to register then confiscate the guns citizens already own. And make no mistake about it, our enforcement agencies would do just that if told to do so by those who pay their salaries. History has long taught that military and governmental enforcers are loyal to the government that pays them and forget their loyalties to the people.

We already see our government using unconstitutional laws to prevent citizens from using their constitutional rights to keep and bear firearms, granted under the second, ninth, and tenth Amendments of our Constitutional. And governmental law enforcement agencies follow their governments orders to enforce these unconstitutional laws, instead of protecting the rights of the people granted by our constitution. Remember the words of our founders; When government is the only one that has guns no citizen is safe, and freedom will not last.

If you believe our rights and liberties are not under assault by our own government consider the path our states, with the endorsement of Washington, has taken. We now see every manner of sting operations undertaken by state and federal enforcement agencies. We all would agree that some of those caught in such operations surely need to be taken out of society. But Sting operations in which no actual victim exists are sending defendants to prison and such actions, however warranted, are unconstitutional.

Random road blocks where citizens are stopped, detained and searched for proof of insurance and sniffed for alcohol consumption, all without probable cause or warrant. Citizens so unconstitutionally stopped, detained and searched may then suffer loss of drivers rights and face fines or imprisonment based upon evidence illegally obtained in violation of our constitutional laws requiring probable cause and warrants. All without probable cause, sufficient to obtain a warrant, as required by our constitution. Was a warrant obtained with the verification of just cause by two witnesses as required by our constitution? While some abuses of citizens rights by the government may seem unimportant, one should remember. Each right and liberty you voluntarily surrender leads you closer to the loss of all rights and liberties. No people ever lost all their rights overnight, they lost them one at a time, one at a time.

I am reminded of the comments of some who survived the extermination camps of Hitler's Germany. When they came for the Jews no one complained, when they came for the elderly no one objected, when they came for the disabled and incompetent no one complained,

When they came for me no one was left to complain. And so it will be in America. If you give up one right they will take another, and another until you have no rights, including the right to own a firearm, and including all your personal rights, liberties and freedoms guaranteed by the constitution our forefathers died to give us.

Consider also, enforcement officers cruise your streets using scanners to listen in on private conversations of citizens using a hand held remote phone while in their own homes. They drive by your homes with heat detectors searching your homes for evidence of illegal activities. They do so without a warrant or probable cause. This is a direct invasion of a citizens rights to privacy in their homes, places and person. This is an unconstitutional practice by which enforcement officers invade the privacy of a citizens home without probable cause or warrant. America now accepts these constitutional violations without questioning their legality.

Consider the unconstitutional actions of New Orleans elected officials and law enforcement officials who invaded the homes of New Orleans citizens during the chaos left by the hurricane and flooding of that city. Once they had entered private homes, without probable cause or warrant, they seized the firearms of private citizens leaving them at the mercy of armed gangs. And those illegally confiscated firearms have never been found and returned to their rightful legal owners. Many states have these unconstitutional laws that permit government to suspend or limit gun sales during periods of emergencies. They are enforced by law enforcement agencies. And they will come for your firearms and render you defenseless when told to do so.

The Socialists and Communists in the United Nations and in Washington are concerned because about forty million citizens in America own firearms, including rifles, shotguns and handguns used for hunting, target shooting and self protection. Washington socialists and the United Nations want the American people to be disarmed. Because these forty million citizens would, if they have the courage to do so, make a formidable army to oppose any complete Washington sell out to the United Nations.

That is why the founders of our nation included the second, ninth and tenth amendments in our Bill of Rights. To give the people the ability to stop a federal army if it ever had to be done. But an armed citizenry must have the courage of our fathers to demand the return of government to the people. Whether they now have that strength and courage is questionable.

Consider also the cry of the Socialists in Washington and from other socialists organizations to limit gun ownership to so called smart guns. Guns that would identify the owner and fire only if held by the owner. No such weapons are currently available and the expense of technology to make them would price a gun above the means of most citizens. Such laws would also require the confiscation of all firearms not meeting the smart gun designs.

Thus with no guns available meeting smart gun requirements, and all other guns not meeting the smart gun requirements confiscated, American citizens would be disarmed and America would be ripe for the taking by the Socialists in our midst and in the United Nations.

Consider how local jurisdictions enact their own unconstitutional ordinances that conflict with state gun laws making criminals out of honest law abiding citizens who have a right to keep and carry guns. Citizens caught up in such a patchwork of rules that vary from state to state, city to city, face enormous expenses trying to clear their name. And the socialists judicial appointees support these unconstitutional actions by state and municipal bodies.

We see efforts by the Socialists in Washington and in our states to force all gun purchasers, and gun owners, to obtain a license and register their firearms. Make no mistake about it, once gun owner licensing and registration is in place, gun confiscation will follow. We have already seen gun registration lists used to confiscate all legally owned firearms in Germany, Greece, Ireland, Great Britain, Australia and other countries. The United Nations treaties, of which America is a part, require this and the Socialists in our country are working to make it happen in America. A disarmed America is their top priority.

It has already happened here in America. In 1967, New York City passed an ordinance requiring citizens to obtain a permit and register their firearms. Then in 1991, the city passed a ban on private ownership of certain semi-automatic firearms- then used the registration lists to require gun owners to remove their guns from the city or surrender them to government officials. Gun registration has been used, and will again be used, to disarm American citizens.

Clearly our governments, federal and state, are circumventing our constitution with their unconstitutional laws and secret treaties with the Communist and Socialists rulers of the United Nations. Their clear intent is the disarming of the America people, and the results of their actions are, whether intentional or out of ignorance, decimating our constitution and our constitutional protections. If successful, the only people with guns will be our military forces and government enforcers. An unarmed, helpless, fearful and apathetic America can then be easily turned over to the United Nations. American sovereignty and American laws and judicial systems will be replaced by United Nations laws and United Nations Socialist controls.

The future of American sovereignty, our constitutional system of laws and the liberties we once enjoyed are at risk. Make no mistake about it. An armed citizenry is all that stands between freedom, as American citizens having constitutionally established laws, or enslavement under United Nations Socialist rule. The United Nations intentions are clear. Their goal is to disarm America as they have done in other countries. The want their armies to be the only people with guns. They will come for your guns. It is only a matter of waiting until their socialist partners in Washington clear the way for them to do so.

I have been in places where the people have no rights. I walked out of Dachau concentration camp, just outside of Munich Germany, more than sixty years ago. But the memory of that terrible place and the canals filled with bodies of the disarmed and helpless haunt me still. With the direction Washington is taking us today, I have to wonder, Will we someday have our Dachau in America? A Dachau filled with the bodies of Christian believers and those who resist Socialist rule.

Only one step is left that stands between freedom or collapse for America, the disarming of the American people. Whether the people can muster the courage to demand a return to constitutional rule and retain our national sovereignty is in doubt. But unless the people can do so, the collapse of America is imminent.

Disarming America

PART TWO, WHAT IS COMING:

It is now time to consider what the future may hold for all America. Will Washington take that last step necessary to complete the abolishment of our Constitution and the Sovereignty of our nation. Part two of this chapter describes the actions government has already taken, and actions I predict government will someday take to disarm the people, and lead our nation into total collapse.

Washington has already taken America over the first seven steps of the eight necessary for our nation to collapse. Our legislators gave themselves the power to seize our earnings and our properties. They joined the unholy United Nations New World Order. They instituted so called welfare and subsidy policies to make all Americans dependent upon government for their livelihood to get their votes. They instituted policies to control the media and what the people hear. They brought globalization and destruction to American industry and decimated our military forces. They have all but prohibited the free expression of our Christian faith. They have all but decimated our constitutional sovereignty.

But before the constitution and bill of rights can be completely abolished the people will have to be disarmed. They are working tirelessly to complete the eighth step necessary to bring about the collapse of America, the disarming of the people. Once this step is accomplished it leaves only the last step, Americas collapse.

America is on the last step of the ladder to collapse. Will the American people take this last step, register then surrender their weapons, and watch America collapse? Is this where it will end for our children and grandchildren?

Constitutional Laws that had been based upon the Christian principles of our Americas founders are under attack from within and from without. Moslem religious leaders who control the United Nations were demanding that they be given authority over their people in the United States. Latino immigrants were demanding they be tried under the laws of their home countries or international law. Could this happen? I predict it will.

United Nations Socialists and communist leaders are demanding that American laws and courts be discarded and all America be brought under the realm of international laws and international criminal and civil courts. They further demanded that the outdated Constitution be replaced by the United Nations Charter and United Nations international treaties that have been enacted. The United Nations argued that the time for national sovereignty and national constitutions had passed and that America give up it's sovereignty and become a state within the United Nations. Could it happen, read on and see.

In 1992 the United Nations adopted their policy, Agenda For Peace, that calls for America to keep a military force ready for the United Nation should they require them. That Agenda For Peace also states the time for absolute and exclusive national sovereignty has passed. There appears little doubt Washington agrees with that agenda because they continue to provide military and economic assistance to the United Nations when they demand it.

The socialists in Washington and the Council on Foreign Relations agreed that it is time to abolish our constitution and the stage was set to make the conversion from national sovereignty to full United Nations membership. But changing the Laws and conversion to United Nations full state membership would require the complete abolishment of the constitution and the rights and liberties it grants the citizens. Opposition was to be expected from some citizens. How serious that opposition might be was uncertain.

I agree opposition and resistance to governments actions to disarm the people will take place, but I believe that resistance will be limited to a small number of citizens. I further predict that the lack of significant opposition will open the way for the Socialists to complete the destruction of America. Here is my prediction of the policies and actions government might take to reach their goal of the destruction of America and gain world dominion.

To insure the socialists could maintain control of all America in future elections the congress agreed to consider a bill submitted by legislators from the state of Maryland. That bill would abolish elections based upon the electoral college system. If adopted the bill would change national presidential elections and declare the candidate who receives the highest number of popular votes nationwide would be declared the winner. If adopted, a candidate could win the presidential election simply by winning the popular vote, even if the candidate only won the seven most populated states heavily populated by welfare recipients and illegal voting immigrants.

After some discussion the full congress voted in favor of the bill then submitted it to the senate for consideration. The senate quickly concurred, passed the bill, then sent it to the president for his signature. The president concurred, signed the bill, and it became the law. With that action completed socialist were guaranteed to control the office of presidency in future elections. Could that happen, time will tell but that bill is under consideration, and I predict it will be done.

Congress then enacted a bill, ratified by the senate and signed by the president, that would require all states to revise their election laws to elect all congressional and senatorial candidates based upon the total popular vote of the state, not by district votes. This insured state candidates for national offices would be selected by the populated cities where welfare money bought votes. Could this happen? Again time will tell, but as I write that bill is under consideration.

By continuing the federal welfare subsidies, free rent, food, housing and medical care to the fifty million people residing in the seven most populated states, the socialist were guaranteed their votes, and now control all future presidential elections. By continuing federal and state welfare subsidies to the heavily populated cities, socialists would also control all future congressional and senatorial elections. The Washington socialists will then be ready to move ahead with policies of disarmament and socialism for America.

Agreement was reached among the various state and federal leaders that disarming the people must be done in stages to avoid a national confrontation between older citizens who grew up believing in their government and those who have already accepted Washington's denial of their constitutional rights. All agreed the most important item of agenda must be the confiscation of all firearms from the civilian populace. Towards that end an all out campaign to convince the people that the level of criminal activity requires all citizens be required to register their firearms. The big lie they made was, that if guns were registered criminals would be barred from owning guns. An apathetic people forgot we already had laws that prevent criminals from owning firearms.

And since the record shows severe punishment of those who commit crimes with firearms has never happened, are we to believe any new law would be enforced any better than laws already on the books? The fact is they won't be enforced any better than current laws. The obvious lack of enforcement would lead any rational person to believe there are some who appreciate high crime rates because it helps further their efforts to disarm all American citizens.

While arguments were ongoing between government and those who believe in their second amendment right to keep and bear firearms, the government was quietly adopting policies that will set the stage for disarming the people. Laws were adopted that required background checks before a firearm could be purchased.

These individual background checks gave the government a record of all who purchased a firearm. That register of firearm purchases and the names and addresses of those who purchased a firearm was now available for all enforcement agencies, and the United Nations registry as well. And never forget, registration is the precursor of confiscation. It has been in every country that disarmed their citizens. Ask the unarmed and helpless people in England. Ask the unarmed and helpless people in Australia.

Laws were adopted that required individuals who wanted to use their constitutional right to keep and carry a firearm first must register, then apply for a permit and submit to a background check. This furnished the government the names of all citizens who chose to comply with the right to carry laws.

Despite the second, ninth and tenth amendments rights of citizens to keep and bear firearms, those who decided not to apply for a permit and who were then caught with a gun were of course arrested and then barred from ever owning a firearm. Thus the government completed another step towards building a registry of gun owners for future use. And an apathetic and fearful people surrendered their rights to own and bear firearms, obtained their permits, and gave government control over another part of their lives After years of constant demands for the banning of private ownership of firearms, and months of propagandizing by Washington and the controlled media, the congress placed into consideration a Bill, which if enacted, would require all citizens to register their firearms.

Of course there was some discussion over the proposed Bill. The Congress had to make it look as if there had been a serious debate. In the end only a handful of legislators from states where hunting and sport shooting was still popular opposed the proposed bill. But most family gatherings for hunting had long ago been replaced with the teachings of atheism and the media promotion of sex and violence in their movies. Opposition came mostly from the older generation, those who had grown up in the Midwest farmlands and southern hills and woodlands.

After a few months of deliberation the Congress passed the bill by a majority vote and it was then sent to the Senate for their consideration. Some months later the Senate, with only the legislators from a dozen states opposing the action, voted to pass the bill. House and Senate leaders then met to establish the effective date for required firearm registration to take effect. It was agreed that the effective date for registration would be established to commence thirty days following the presidential signing and approving the bill into law. After a few weeks of posturing the president signed the bill and it became the law of the land.

The people of America now had thirty days to decide whether to submit to the dictates of a socialist government or fight to preserve their constitutional rights and liberties. Registration centers had been established in every county, city, town and village across America where citizens were ordered to comply with the law and register their firearms.

Representatives of federal and state agencies and law enforcement agencies from state, county and city were all in attendance the day registration was scheduled to commence. This would be a week long event to insure all citizens were given time to comply with the law.

When that fateful day arrived for the forced registration of all firearms, Washington and the world waited to see the events unfold. All state national guard units across the country had been placed on alert with orders to respond should it become necessary. But there was little opposition from the people. To the disgrace of all Americans and American history, tens of millions of citizens drove and walked to the county courthouses to register their firearms. Walking like sheep blindly following the edits of their Socialists leaders. Many of the More courageous citizens, however, ignored the laws and refused to register their firearms.

After months of registering processes, and periods of amnesty granted to those who had failed to register initially, the process was continued. Some citizens, however, still did not comply and register their firearms as required and no actions were taken to force those citizens to comply. It was believed the number of citizens who followed governments orders to register their firearms indicated the vast majority of the people had complied.

As time went by other matters were widely publicized. The sporadic racial violence and tensions between religious factions and so called crime on the streets was used to build the case for gun confiscation. The need to disarm the people was proclaimed by Washington and continuously broadcast over the controlled media.

The Washington Socialists working thru their parent organization, The Council on Foreign Relations, kept the pressure on Washington to act to remove all guns from the hands of the people. The Communists and Socialists leaders of the United Nations continued their quest for world dominion, demanding Washington live up to international treaties that prohibit ownership of firearms by private citizens. The push for gun controls and confiscation by the controlled liberal monopoly of media, radio and press in America went on without letup and few opposing viewpoints were heard over the controlled media.

The National Rifle Association, and it's membership, long the strongest defenders of the constitutional right of American citizens to own guns for hunting and sport shooting, had demanded the supreme court stop the registration processes and rule the law unconstitutional. But their ability to reach the people and impress the court was limited and restricted to their own publications and a few radio broadcasters. Although it was estimated that upwards of forty million citizens were gun owners, only a small portion of those, five million, were actual National Rifle Association members. And like the Americans of Christian faith, the number of National Association members were not sufficient to have serious influence on the Socialist now running things in Washington.

The National Rifle Association was coming under attack by the media and Socialist legislators in Washington, claiming it to be encouraging citizen disobedience and civil disrespect for law.

The Congress was debating whether membership in an organization that fosters disrespect for the law should become a crime, and eventually did adopt a formal declaration establishing the National Rifle Association as a subversive organization. While waiting for the Federal Attorney General office and the courts to decide on the legality of their declaration, the Congress introduced legislation that would make it a crime to publicly encourage citizens to refuse to comply with Federal laws. That Bill was passed by both houses of the Congress then signed into law by the President. Could this happen? I have no doubt it will one day.

Following the enactment of the law that branded National Rifle Association executives as criminals, The National Rifle Association was ordered to disband and membership in the National Rifle Association became a criminal offense. The National Rifle Association was directed to provide the government with the names of all current and past members then disband. Immediately National Rifle Association executives and staff commenced to destroy all membership records and all other records containing information that could disclose a members name.

Federal agents stormed the National Rifle Association offices to prevent the destruction of membership records. But the president of the association had at one point declared the only way government would collect his gun was from his cold dead hands, and he had meant it.He and his staff had secured their weapons preparing for this day. Gunfights erupted in National Rifle Association office complexes as executives and staff tried to fight off government agents. Then hundreds of Armed citizens came to the assistance of National Rifle Association executive officers and staff members and gunfights commenced inside and outside the NRA offices. Federal officers were badly outnumbered and those who survived the fighting dropped their weapons and ran. National Rifle Association officers and staff continued the destruction of all records containing the names of their membership.

Thousands of Federal and State military forces dispatched to supplement state, local and federal enforcement personnel arrived at the location and firefights between those forces and civilian protestors took on the look of a battlefield confrontation.

But the overwhelming numbers of Federal military forces far outnumbered those defending their rights. After several days of house to house firefights the citizens forces were surrounded by overwhelming numbers of Federal forces and found themselves being badly beaten. Those who were able to escape did so and after a week of fighting the battle was over.

Independent gun rights groups throughout the Midwest and some southern states were also attempting to organize the people into resisting government gun registration laws. But fear of government persecution and prosecution forced many citizens, who had not yet done so, to register their firearms. America was becoming a nation of fearful people submitting to the laws of socialist tyrants. But there were others, although relatively few in numbers, who refused to surrender their rights and liberties and vowed to resist to the end.

Sadly, most citizens remembered what happened to the National Rifle Association executive officers and friends when they resisted government orders, and feared what might happen if they refused to comply with government laws. America was becoming a nation of people who let fear guide their lives. Families were divided and communities no longer assembled together to honor the faith of their fathers.

The socialists in government kept up their constant nationwide propaganda campaign to convince the people that only by removing firearms from the hands of all could their safety be secured. The controlled media responded and continued for months to report the inflated crime numbers and sell the need to remove firearms from the hands of dangerous criminals and reckless citizens. Never speaking the truth that the majority of violent crimes were committed by a few who chose to act like the animals they believed they descended from. Other criminal activities, atrocities committed by organized anti gun groups, became common. Opposition to the governments campaign to disarm the people was seldom heard and never reported by the media.

Believing the will of the people had been broken Washington enacted the fateful law. The Congress debated then passed a bill and sent it to the senate for their consideration. That bill stated, there was no constitutional citizens right to ownership of firearms. In the opinions of the socialist congress it was claimed, Citizens are entitled to those rights granted by their government, dependent upon conditions that exist today, not the rights granted by a paper issued more than two hundred years earlier. After a few days of discussions and mock debates the senate upheld the congressional bill and sent it to the president for his signature. The president signed the Bill and that law was then upheld by Socialist appointees in the Federal Supreme Court, and became the law of the land.

Immediately a Federal Decree was issued, and the Socialist controlled media gladly broadcast and printed the orders from Washington. Ownership of firearms, of any kind, make or description by private citizens was now prohibited. All States, Counties and Municipalities were ordered to establish firearm collection stations. Once these stations were established, all privately owned firearms were to be surrendered to government authorities immediately. A date was established for the national confiscation of all citizen owned firearms to commence.

When ready and opened the collection stations were manned with Federal enforcement personnel, State and local authorities and United Nations observers. The day had arrived. America was to be disarmed. The fate of all America was at hand. Freedom for all Americans hung in the balance.

Would the people comply or resist in the name of liberty. Sadly, fear of government had become a controlling emotion for many American citizens.

And so they came to the collection stations, slowly at first, carrying the firearms they had used for hunting and sport shooting. At most locations little or no resistance was seen. In some locations across the country it was reported scattered problems had erupted.

Bands of dissidents attacked the enforcers at collections stations and it appeared opposition was commencing to take place. State National Guard forces were being transported to those areas to fight the dissidents.

Running firefights commenced at many locations and government threw thousands of active duty military personnel into the actions to put these local resistance groups down and avoid a national uprising. But opposition forces seemed to be growing in several states where veterans and those who loved hunting were refusing to turn their weapons in.

But before the decision was made to require the people to surrender their firearms, government had recalled all military forces home from the many countries where they had been stationed. Although decimated by years of no win United Nations wars, the military was still a formidable force. When compared to what appeared to be small numbers of resistors.

Wherever resistors confronted the government enforcers, hundreds of military personnel were thrown into the regions to stamp out the dissident forces. But still they fought on defending their rights and liberties. Mostly they were the older citizens who had once known freedom and who now fought for their liberties.

Within months wherever small company sized dissident forces made contact with local and state forces they were soon facing thousands of active military forces.

Resistors facing such overwhelming odds were being mercilessly slaughtered in battles. Many of the survivors and wounded dissidents who were captured alive were summarily executed as traitors where they were taken prisoner. The socialist controlled media used all their dirty tactics to throw fear into the minds of the people. They took care to record and show only the bodies of the dissidents who were killed and took particular care to show the summary executions of captured dissidents.

But despite the odds and barbaric treatment of prisoners resistance continued and the number of dissidents grew in some states. At some rural communities across the country the intense fighting resembled battlefield conditions. People were coming out of the hills in large numbers and joining their fellow men in battle. These battles waged on for months until it seemed the dissidents would surely run out of weapons and ammunition to fight.

But the people were determined and taking weapons and ammunition from the bodies of government forces in many instances to continue their fight for freedom.

Other bands of citizens were attacking and raiding lightly manned national guard armories to re-supply their fellow men engaged in the battles for liberty. These battles were mostly confined to the mid-west and southern states bordering on the old mason and Dixon line. Citizens along the west coast, southern coastal states and east and north eastern coastal states had long ago became so indoctrinated in government policies they had forgotten their loyalties to America or their friends and fellow citizens.

In some places dissidents began attacking government offices and the homes of government leaders with home made bombs and grenades. Law enforcement officers considered traitors of the people became targets of opportunity for the resistance fighters. These actions helped draw the military away from resistance field units. Small military convoys were attacked and ambushed as the resistance forces began organizing into smaller groups making it more difficult for large military units to track them.

The army began bringing in helicopter gunships to support the government forces. But in the close hand to hand combat conditions these gun-ships were killing as many of their own as they were dissidents. In municipalities such tactics were taking a heavy toll on the lives of citizens, many of whom had given up their firearms. But there was no outcry about the ongoing slaughter of innocent people from the leaders of the United Nations and it's member states.

In Midwest America small bands of dissidents had grown to hundreds and in some places thousands. It was no longer safe for local and county law enforcement personnel to move on the roads and streets without military support due to citizens attacking them.

National guard companies reinforced by active military units were now heavily involved in trying to suppress the rebelling citizens.

Throughout the Midwest roving bands of citizens were attacking government personnel. Many of these citizens had seen military service in Viet Nam and the Persian gulf conflicts. They had learned from the tactics of the enemies there and were using those same tactics against government forces. Their primary targets were government supply convoys where supplies of weapons and ammunition could be taken and furnished larger elements for the ongoing battles against government forces.

With little or no resistance occurring in the other regions of the country most military forces stationed in those states were being relocated to the Midwest heartland states to reinforce government forces encountering strong resistance. The larger battles were now taking place throughout Ohio, Kentucky and West Virginia. It was becoming apparent that many citizens had not turned in all their firearms and ammunition. But with most of their supplies now coming from raids on enemy supply convoys many wondered how long the fighting could last.

Government officials were reporting that thousands of the dissidents had been killed and many others wounded and that the fighting would soon be over. But reports from sources close to the fighting were saying government losses far exceeded the losses expected, that thousands had been lost in Ohio alone with thousands more casualties being suffered throughout the heartland of America. These reports were then used to urge United Nations military forces into the fight.

Government forces had moved hundreds of low flying aircraft and helicopters into the heartland to provide more intense firepower for their armies when engaged with citizens forces. Their use prevented the citizens forces from engaging the military in large battles and they suffered heavy losses when caught in the open. In some areas the capability of dissident forces to meet the military in head on battles had been critically weakened.

In Indiana government forces had caught resistance forces in large numbers on several instances and Indiana resistors were moving into Ohio to link up with resistance forces.

The heaviest fighting was now centered in the states of Ohio, West Virginia, Pennsylvania and northern Kentucky where citizens forces had rebelled in larger numbers. In the hills and mountains of those states Government forces were unable to get into position to meet the citizens forces in large battles. The dissidents picked the time and place for most encounters and used surprise and hit and run tactics to their advantage. The longer the resistance lasted their numbers increased and the fighting intensified.

It had now been nearly a year since government forces had been turned loose upon the citizens of America. From their vantage point it was clear that heavy losses in manpower and supply shortages had taken their toll on the citizens forces. Because of their inability to reinforce their ranks and re-supply their forces they could no longer stand and fight the military. Their capability was now limited to ambush and hit and run tactics. The resistance forces were in trouble in Northern Kentucky where state and local forces outnumbered the resistance.

The world waited and watched wondering how long the dissident forces could withstand such overwhelming military might. The people of France, England, Australia, Belgium and the Netherlands had twice been saved from extinction by American armies during World Wars One and Two. But not one of these countries came to the assistance of the American citizens. In fact, they were beyond being able to help for all had already surrendered their sovereignty and weapons to become member states of the United Nations.

In an all out effort to break the back of resistance forces one hundred thousand federal forces waiting in reserve were flown in and dropped into the Ohio, northern Kentucky and West Virginia regions. Thousands more were transported by rail and troop carriers reinforcing federal forces in those states. Many of these units were accompanied by United Nations military advisors. Even the sight of these foreign green uniformed forces invading their country failed to incite the people into action. Years of national apathy had led to the destruction of the American dream. Fear of government had long ago replaced love of country.

Large battles between the resistors and federal forces were becoming less and less frequent and once engaged military aircraft strafing and helicopter gunship rockets added to overwhelming numbers of ground forces were inflicting heavy losses on the isolated citizens forces. But still they fought on using the tactics of ambush, hit and raid to secure needed equipment and supplies. Lessons many of these veterans had learned serving their country during the conflicts in Viet Nam and the Mid- East. Now they fought and died because their hearts would not allow them to surrender and face enslavement.

In Kentucky where an estimated fifty thousand federal forces had moved in resistors were being destroyed and scattered elements were being eliminated. Surviving resistors from Kentucky were straggling into Ohio and West Virginia to join their fellow patriots and continue their fight. The conflict became a series of running battles as dissenters kept on the move selecting their targets, trying to isolate smaller units. Small army units were attacked in their base camps by dissident patrols, then ambushes were set up to strike larger governments units coming to relieve the base camps under attack. It was Viet Nam all over again, except it was now taking place on American soil.

The total number of resistors in Ohio now was estimated to number several thousand and their numbers in West Virginia were considered even higher. The Ohio resistance force was gaining strength from Pennsylvania where thousands had moved to join their Ohio friends. Large numbers of government military personnel had moved in to fight that force but were being outmaneuvered by the local citizens who knew the territory well. Federal forces were suffering large numbers of casualties and dissident forces were seizing guns, ammunition, other supplies and food from the federal unit's they met in battle.

In West Virginia the resistance numbers were increased by the flow of resistors moving in from the state of Virginia. Thousands of Federal forces had been moved into the area but were suffering large numbers of casualties from the dedicated fighters there. Resistors were attacking federal supply columns and securing needed firearms, ammunition and supplies. Clearly the federal commands had underestimated the numbers of dissident citizens. As word spread of the fighting outbreaks of resistance was increasing in other states across the country.

In several states resistors had attacked and taken over national guard centers seizing the arms, ammunition and rations stored there and were transporting it to the resisters where the intense fighting was taking place. With reinforcements coming in from Pennsylvania and Virginia resistance forces were making the federal armies pay a heavy price in personnel and equipment. Federal air and ground forces had for half a century been scattered around the world fighting no win wars for the United Nations. Their numbers, already decimated by socialist programs had reduced the overall size of the military, were now being reduced even farther in the fighting to control the rebellion.

But federal armies still outnumbered resistance forces in the contested states and fear kept most citizens from joining their countrymen in their fight for liberty. The major media still operating kept up a steady barrage of reporting federal successes in the battles. Trying to convince the people resistance was useless in order to reduce the number of citizens willing to risk their lives for freedom. Except for slight resistance in the northwest states the fighting was now centered in the Ohio, West Virginia and Kentucky region. It was becoming clear that federal forces were superior in numbers and equipment to the resistance fighters. Experts wondered how long the outnumbered resistors could continue the fighting.

Then, three years after the rebellion commenced, the fighting was over. There was no surrender. Survivors laid down their arms and melted away into the hills and woods to avoid capture and certain death from the military. Many did so believing there would come another time when more of their countrymen would find the will to defend their liberties. It was later determined that forty thousand citizens had honored the legacy handed down by their forefathers.

Forty thousand had followed the words of Patrick Henry "I know not what course others may follow, but as for myself, give me liberty or give me death". Sadly, except for those few of courage, a once proud and mighty people had surrendered their rights, freedom and liberties voluntarily to a corrupt socialist government.

THE COLLAPSE OF AMERICA

In my book I have identified eight steps, policy decisions, that will lead to the collapse of America. I have described what has been done, where we are today, and where I believe the future will take us. Step 1, a Constitutional amendment giving Congress the power to seize our earnings by taxing them has been completed. Step 2, joining the United Nations has been accomplished. Step 3, creating a socialist welfare state has been accomplished. Step 4, creating a controlled media has been accomplished. Step 5, destroying our industrial base has been accomplished.

Step 6, Abolishing our constitution, The constitution has been decimated, and has become meaningless. Should national collapse occur, constitutional rule will end. Step 7, The Destruction of our Christian base is nearly complete. Step 8, The Disarming of America now awaits only the election of sufficient numbers of liberal socialists, and the appointment of their liberal jurists, to complete the disarmament. In this chapter I have described the actions, I predict, government will take to complete the destruction of our constitution, The destruction of our Christian base and the disarmament of the people. I have described the future events, that I predict, will take place leading to the final and total collapse of America.

The events described in the following pages, while fictional will, I believe, follow the economic and military decline and the destruction of every principle that our country was founded upon.

The influx of immigrants and granting them rights to vote completed the destruction of the Christian voting base. Welfare giveaways to the immigrants added to the millions already living off taxpayers earnings gave a large voting block to the socialist party. That led to the socialists supporting a candidate for president whose national and religious loyalties were suspect, certainly not in the tradition of the founding fathers. A candidate who, although born an American, had been raised by Moslem parents and educated in Moslem schools overseas.

That candidate was swooned over by the socialist controlled media and his known and alleged associations with anti American and Moslem leaders were not reported nor discussed by the main media. A few radio talk show hosts did report on his associations however these programs reached relatively few of the total voting citizens. The left wing socialist already in office threw their support behind their candidate and other socialist running for congressional seats as well. Before long the people would be faced with the results of their apathy and malaise and their love for a free hand out.

For months following the end of conflict the people went about the business of locating missing family members and burying those who had given their all for freedom. Washington too was busy returning the bodies of their dead to family members. Many however, both federal and dissident fighters, had been buried in mass makeshift graves. Many others lie decomposed where they fell. Government workers and the military erected temporary incinerator stations at several locations and commenced the work of disposing of the thousands of bodies. These sites took on the appearance of the German death camps and the odors permeated the air for miles around. Tens of thousands of families would never see their loved ones again.

The new President and Congress addressed the people over those communication medias still functional calling for calm. Peace has been restored they said, America must unite now and go forward with confidence in the future. State and local officials also were trying to restore calm to their communities. But in many communities state enforcement officers were not welcome in their communities. Memories of their betrayal of the people had not been forgotten. Peace and confidence in the future would not soon return to America. Fear of government was the prevailing emotion throughout most families and their searching for food was a never ending problem.

Government was telling the people to remain calm that medical facilities and services as well as the public school system would soon be restored. But with most people unemployed and without funds to pay the cost, restoration of medical facilities and services would be useless.

Washington announced that these medical services would be staffed and operated by government employed medical personnel, and Washington assured the people that all would receive medical care.

Then the Washington socialists announced a program to nationalize all agriculture lands, and to provide jobs to the public, getting food crops planted and harvested. Once those programs were in effect and producing crops, food would be available for all. But everyone knew what that would mean. Millions of illegal immigrants would now be put to work on the farmlands of America encouraging millions more to enter the country. And soon their fears were realized. Socialism had come to America.

Many small farms owners who had not yet been foreclosed on were resisting and the modern day carpetbaggers who had taken over millions of acres of foreclosed farmlands joined in and voiced their resistance to governments intentions to nationalize their land. Government tried to convince these landowners they would be compensated for their losses, but few believed that would ever come to be. Many citizens were now regretting their failure to resist government's seizure of their guns and regretted their failure to join those who had lost their lives resisting government's actions.

Washington and other socialists in the offices of the New York Council on Foreign Relations were growing concerned about the spreading resistance to their socialistic policies and programs. They had thought the worst was over, that resistance had been quelled, and they could proceed at full speed to implement their policies. The president invited then met with leaders of the United Nations. After several days of discussions The President and the United Nations leaders went to the halls of congress to address the legislature. Meetings were then held with the leaders of the Congress. Clearly the president was asking for guarantees of United Nations military assistance if it was needed.

After getting assurances from the United Nations delegates that military assistance was available if needed, the congress decided, and the president agreed, that the time had come for America to surrender it's sovereignty and become a full member of the world governing body.

For weeks Washington, thru their controlled media, attempted to sell the people on the idea that joining the United Nations as a full participating member would benefit all Americans and the world. But opposition was growing across the land in many states.

Finally, in the face of what they believed to be minimal opposition, the Congress voted to consider a bill that would abolish the constitution, including all the Bill of Rights Amendments. It would abolish our national sovereignty. The former Free people would henceforth be governed by the policies of the United Nations charter. It further required that the state and national constitutional laws now followed by the American judicial system be replaced by the laws governing the international criminal and civil courts. There it was, the socialistic proposed destruction of Everything America was built upon.

After a week of discussions and mock debates, the Congress took the bill to the floor for a vote. Within hours the bill was passed and sent to the senate. Only seventeen Congressional members voted against the bill, Seventeen members of Congress wanted America to remain a free sovereign nation governed by a constitution. After one day of discussions in the senate the bill was put to the floor for a vote. The senate ratified the bill with only fourteen senators voting against it's adoption. The bill was submitted to the president for his signature and it was signed into law that same day and it became the law of the land.

Then something totally unexpected happened. Fourteen states jointly declared their independence and announced they were succeeding from the United States of America. In their joint announcement they stated their firm resolve to become a separate union of states. Those state leaders declared they could no longer support a government that had abolished all citizens rights and liberties. They would no longer support a government that taxed the people into indebtedness then used those revenues to commit citizens to fight in no win United Nations wars. They would no longer support a government that had rigged the elective processes to insure they would control all power in the federal governing bodies. I ask you, could this happen? Is there yet strength in the American people to resist enslavement or extermination?

Within days flags containing seventeen stars were seen flying from the housetops in Maine, Massachusetts, New Hampshire, New Jersey, Delaware, Pennsylvania, Michigan, Wisconsin, Iowa, Kansas, Missouri, Illinois, Virginia and Indiana.

The states of Ohio, West Virginia, and Kentucky, where the people had been ravaged by federal forces still had the flame of liberty in them and joined the other states, making a total of seventeen states declaring their independence.

The independent states recalled their army, air force and marine guard units which had been released from federal service at the close of fighting the insurrection. The guard bases were secured to protect the guns, ammunition, equipment and supplies located in them. Wherever there was a shortage of personnel citizens moved in to help secure the installations and supplies. Most state national guard forces all declared their loyalty to their independent home states and citizens forces were being organized by the guard units in every state that had declared their independence.

Washington was threatening military action unless the states renounced their declarations and vowed their allegiance to the United States. But all seventeen states reaffirmed their intentions to withdraw from the United States and form their own union of free democratic states. Leaders around the world wondered if this was the beginning of a second war of independence in America. But while other states had not declared their independence, many in those states agreed with the independent states, but sadly their fear of Washington and the federal armies kept them from joining with the independent states.

Because of the unrest in the state of Virginia, and to a lesser extent in Maryland, The president and congressional legislators who supported the abolishment of national sovereignty and constitutional government were evacuated from the capital city area and relocated on the large air base in Florida for their security.

Other legislators from the states declaring their independence had already left the capital and returned to their home states. There seemed little chance of avoiding military conflict.

The Federal armies had suffered considerable losses in manpower and equipment in the three years of fighting the citizens forces, but without question they were still better equipped and far outnumbered the independent forces.

United Nations leaders called a meeting of the security council to discuss the situation in America. It was decided they would commence to assemble and transport army and air units from other member states to Canada where they would be available to intervene when the time was right.

The United Nations military staff committee ordered three million military personnel to immediately assemble and depart for Canada. Within days United Nations armies, comprised of Asian and Eastern European Moslem forces began arriving in Canada. Their arrival gave the President and Congressional socialists, now headquartered in Florida, confidence United Nations armies would be available if needed.

The president then issued an ultimatum to the states declaring their independence to renounce their unlawful declaration of independence or face military actions. The states refused to comply and continued their preparations for war. Federal armies with light air support began moving out of California, Texas and Oregon attacking citizens forces in Iowa, Kansas and Wisconsin. At the same time federal forces advanced north from the Carolinas and Georgia attacking citizens forces in the eastern border states. Other federal forces moved north from Tennessee and Louisiana attacking the independent forces in Missouri and Illinois. Federal forces moving out of Tennessee and Alabama were probing Kentucky and West Virginia .The battle lines were drawn and the armies were committed and civil war two had begun.

But if federal forces had expected light resistance they soon found they faced a formidable army on all fronts. After several weeks fighting on the western front federal forces had made advances into Iowa and Kansas where Independent forces lacked the equipment to use air power. On the Eastern front Former Federal air power from bases in Virginia were now at the disposal of independent forces, and their army was well organized and equipped. The federal central command moving north from Tennessee and Louisiana expecting the recent fighting had destroyed much of the capability of Kentucky, West Virginia and Ohio people to fight, found a very formidable and determined force opposing them.

Air power from Ohio bases was being used to support independent forces in Kentucky and West Virginia and a real battle was taking place in that region. On the eastern front federal armies were advancing into Virginia and Maryland but the fighting was fierce and casualties were mounting. With federal forces controlling the western and southern borders clearly Washington was intent on taking control of the northeastern independent states to shut off all access to coastal borders and seaports. If successful the independent states would find themselves encircled on the east, west and south with the borders of Canada on the north.

Commanders of the independent forces ordered the state of Pennsylvania to move all their forces south to strengthen their forces in Ohio, West Virginia and Kentucky. New York independent forces were moving east and south to help stop the federal army advance in Virginia and Maryland. Battles were raging on the western front. The federal army supported by air power had pushed deep into Iowa and Kansas and were battering outnumbered independent forces without letup. Independent forces from Wisconsin and Illinois were moving to bring field rations and support for their allies on the western front.

Casualties were mounting for both armies but clearly the independents were taking a beating and being forced to retreat. Independent armed forces with air support were driving federal forces from Tennessee and Louisiana out of Ohio, Kentucky and West Virginia. Those federal units were now trying to maneuver east to unite with their eastern army but were being pounded by independent forces as they retreated.

The addition of the independent army from New York joining with and bringing additional field rations and supplies to other friendly forces had slowed the advance of federal armies on the eastern front. Those armies were now engaged in fierce fighting along the eastern coastal states of New Jersey, Massachusetts and eastern New York state. The media was now reporting that federal forces on the southern and eastern fronts were nearly united into one army and would destroy independent forces. On the western front the media reported additional federal troops had been transported south from Oregon, Washington and Montana to bring supplies and increase federal troop strength in that battle.

Independent forces from Indiana were ordered to move to the western front and began the move to transport additional rations and supplies. This additional thirty thousand troops and supplies were badly needed by their troops engaged in that fight who were facing overpowering numbers of federal troops. Independent air force personnel flying out of the former federal air base in Ohio, and the former federal army base in Kentucky, were doing all they could to re-supply their people on the western and eastern fronts with cargo flights and air drops. Food and equipment stored in those bases were adequate to keep independent forces well supplied.

The fighting had raged on all three fronts for more than a year with casualties heavy on both armies. On the eastern front federal forces from the south had united with the eastern force. But the addition of independent forces from Pennsylvania had stopped the advance of the federal army. Independent forces from the south had closed on the southern flank of the federal army and New York independent forces were holding the western flank. With Independent forces closing on the northern flank, federal forces were now surrounded in the states of New Jersey and Massachusetts and Maryland and outnumbered by independent forces. The federal army was in trouble. Casualties were growing and supplies were running low.

On the western front federal forces had advanced into Missouri but their advance had been stopped with addition of the Wisconsin, Illinois and Indiana independent divisions. These forces had moved in on the northern flanks of federal forces who were now forced to fight on two fronts. The media was now reporting that federal forces were in trouble on all fronts and suffering higher casualties than independent armies. Clearly the federal socialist leaders had underestimated the numbers and capabilities of independent forces.

United Nations leaders had thus far stayed out of the war. They were content to let the American armies, federal and independents, expend themselves and their supplies. They wanted both armies weakened and decimated unable to offer resistance when the time came to move their armies into America. But they had plans ready to put their armies into the fight when the right time came.

The fighting on all three fronts had intensified as independent forces now had the federal armies encircled and were attacking on all fronts. Independent air power had intercepted federal aircraft and destroyed their ability to transport supplies to their troops. Federal armies were running short of supplies and sustaining heavy casualties. Federal government leaders now holed up in Florida were in contact with their field army command urging them to continue the fighting until all independent forces were eliminated. But these commands and their forces were now fighting for survival.

Both armies, independent and federal, were sustaining heavy casualties and media experts were estimating that one half of the forces, both federal and independent, had died in the fighting. Total loss of life was estimated at more than three hundred thousand federal troops and possibly as many independent fighters had lost their lives. It was now believed that the total number of federal troops fighting in both sectors numbered less than three hundred thousand.

The total number of independent forces could only be estimated since there was no way of knowing the total number involved at the beginning.

The war had now been going on for more than three years. America was a decimated country. The industries that had survived globalization policies were shut down. Agricultural production was at a level before the great agricultural revolution, almost nonexistent. There was no mass transportation and air facilities were closed. Public utilities had collapsed in many places and many cities and towns were without power. Schools were a thing of the past and people were without food, water and everyday necessities. Government, even at the local level, was non existent.

Millions of immigrants from Mexico and other Central American states were fleeing the country. They had immigrated to America to escape starvation and poverty, they now found conditions in America worse than those of their home countries. Now, without any means of transportation, waves and droves by the tens of millions of men, women and children could be seen walking in long lines towards the southwest and crossing the border back into Mexico. Central American trucks and busses by the hundreds commenced to enter the country and were assisting their fellow citizens out of the country to escape the carnage. In Canada United Nations leaders had been closely monitoring the struggle across the border. After discussions with other member states around the world, it was agreed, the time had come to enter the war and bring America into complete compliance with United Nations policies. The Military Staff Committee issued the orders to United Nations military commanders.

One million armed soldiers, with air and artillery support. Were ordered to advance south out of Canada thru Wisconsin and end the fighting now centered in the state of Illinois. Another one million armed soldiers, with full air and ground support, were ordered to advance out of Canada thru the states of Maine and New York, and enter the fighting now centered in the states of New Jersey, Maryland, and eastern Pennsylvania. United Nations leaders in Europe and Asia were then directed to commence moving another two million man military force to Canada where they would be held in reserve.

And so they came. A million man army, clad in the green United Nations uniforms, entered American territory in Michigan and began the move towards the fighting in Illinois. Another million green clad soldiers entered American territory and commenced the move thru Maine and New York towards the fighting in the east coast states. Hundreds of low flying aircraft and choppers were held in reserve in Canada. American citizens, stood and watched as the green clad armies moved thru their towns and country sides, unable to believe what was happening. The socialist controlled media, that was still capable of broadcasting, was informing the people to be calm, peace would be restored to their country.

The Washington socialists holed up in Florida had been unable to advise their armies of the United Nations decision to enter the war. They and the Independent forces were unaware of the events unfolding out of Canada and the fighting continued between federal armies and independent forces. Contact by the United

Nations army was made on the western front first. But it was not the actions Washington had expected, or then again, maybe it was. Their first contact was in the form of a heavy surface to surface ground missile barrage followed by low level strafing and bombing by United Nations air attacks flying out of Canadian airfields.

These attacks killed hundreds of federal forces as well as independent forces. The same attacks were carried out by United Nations army and air forces on the eastern front. Again, these attacks killed hundreds of federal as well as independent forces. On the western front United Nations ground armies began attacking from the north and east of the battlefield sector, attacking both independent and federal forces. On the eastern front United Nations ground armies commenced attacking from the north and west, attacking both federal and independent forces.

Communications between field commands of both the federal and independent armies led to a joining of their forces to fight this new threat to their existence. The attacks upon both the federal and independent forces resulted in a merger of independent and federal forces into a much more powerful army on both fronts.

Federal soldiers now realized the goal of United Nations leaders was to eliminate all military capability of the American people, not just the independent forces. But their awakening to the intentions of Washington socialists and United Nations leaders may have come to late. With the two million United Nations forces being held in reserve clearly they outnumbered all American forces. Independent air force planes flying out of Ohio commenced bombing the United Nations forces on the western front and fighters intercepted and destroyed several United Nations aircraft.

On the eastern front independent air force pilots flying out of Virginia bases began intercepting United Nations aircraft destroying many of their aircraft. At the same time federal and independent chopper pilots flying out of Virginia commenced attacking United Nations forces with missile attacks and strafing operations.

The state leaders of the independent states contacted their field commanders on both fronts and recommended they break out of their positions and move towards eastern Ohio and West Virginia and unite into one larger force. At the same time they called upon every citizen in their states to arm themselves and fight a harassing action against United Nations forces attacking the retreating independent forces. Commanders agreed the relocation and uniting of armies would give them more capability to fight the United Nations army on the ground and bring the fighting closer to their air capabilities in Ohio.

Believing they had the American forces on the run United Nations armies pursued the retreating forces but in doing so exposed themselves to attacks by independent aircraft and harassment from local citizens. It took several weeks for the independent and federal armies to complete the relocation and unite, but once completed they now had a powerful army under one united command. The battleground now was centered in Ohio, Kentucky and Indiana. American forces had the munitions and armor from the Fort Knox post and the Ohio air base under their control and were well supplied to continue the fighting.

But the numerical strength of the United Nations army was such that the Americans used a tactic of attacking then retreating rather than try to overwhelm the foreign army. The fighting raged on for months and the united American armies were slowly pushing the United Nations forces into northern Ohio and lower Michigan. United Nations forces were sustaining heavy losses from ground and air attacks and were approaching full retreat.

But United Nations leaders in Canada were monitoring the conditions on the ground by flyovers and communications with field commanders. They ordered one million troops to proceed south thru Wisconsin and Indiana and attack the west flank of the American army. At the same time another one million troops were ordered to move south thru western Pennsylvania and attack the American army from their eastern flank. These troop movements took several weeks to complete but once in place they attacked the encircled American army from the north, west and east.

Now facing superior numbers and firepower the American armies could either retreat south or hold their positions and make the enemy forces pay a heavy price for every inch of ground they gave up. They chose the latter and committed themselves to fighting until there was no one left to carry the American flag. The independent central command decided they would not make it easy for the United Nations armies.

They ordered all their forces to launch an all out attack against the enemy forces on the west. And so they did, driving the enemies to their west back into Indiana and inflicting heavy losses on them. After one month they turned and attacked the armies on the east driving them towards the state of Pennsylvania and inflicting heavy losses on them.

Then after a month they turned and launched an all out attack again to the west. These maneuvers caused heavy losses to the enemy forces being attacked, but just as important they made it difficult for trailing enemy forces to keep them encircled or close on their force from all sides.

Then the independent central command requested and received an approximate number each field commander had. The eastern command from Pennsylvania reported he had approximately one hundred thousand personnel capable of fighting. The western command from Arizona and Wisconsin reported they had approximately sixty thousand personnel remaining able to fight. The southern command from Ohio, Kentucky and West Virginia reported their remaining force consisted of approximately forty thousand personnel.

After discussing their options the central command made a decision they hoped would cause the enemy the most problems and casualties. They were encircled by enemy forces to their north, east and west, leaving the south flank open.

All field commands were ordered to move directly south at full retreat for two days. Then the western command was to turn and head west at full speed. They were to try to get outside the enemy forces and attack them from the west. The eastern command also was to head south for two days then turn and attack enemy forces from the east. The southern command was ordered to hold their positions and fight a delaying action. This was hoped it would convince enemy forces to keep pressing their attack from their current positions giving the east and west commands time to maneuver into position to attack the enemy from the east and west.

Their plans proved to be successful and within weeks American forces launched attacks against the enemy from the east and west. These unexpected operations inflicted heavy casualties on the enemy forces. United Nations leaders, believing new additional American armies had increased the strength of the army they were fighting, ordered their reserve forces in Canada to prepare to move south to reinforce their ranks.

The American central command received reports of the United Nations build up in Canada and discussed what actions to take. It was decided, and agreed to by all commanders, that their only option was to attack the enemy build up from the air. They ordered all their fighter bomber aircraft to prepare to attack. They were advised they had six remaining aircraft capable of attacking the enemy forces in Canada. The decision was made. Three aircraft were to attack the enemy force facing them in Ohio, Illinois and eastern Pennsylvania. They were advised to load their planes to capacity with bombs, one was to hit the enemy on the east, one on the west, and another was to hit the main enemy force central positions in Ohio.

The other three aircraft were to fly into the Canadian border positions where the enemy were commencing their move south. They were ordered to each load as many five thousand pound cluster bombs as their planes could carry. Then drop their full load of bombs at several locations along the Canadian border. After dropping his cluster bombs, One plane was to drop one ten thousand pound blockbuster bomb on the bridge between Canada and Michigan. That would force them to move to Wisconsin or Pennsylvania to cross the lakes into America, and put them several weeks away from the main battle site.

Those forces that had already started their move south would be cut off from their main force, and the main force would be stopped where they were. All agreed their actions were necessary, that America was doomed to be abolished, and the people enslaved under United Nations rule if they failed to stop the enemy advance. All aircraft crews were advised once their orders were carried out to return to the Ohio base, if at all possible, and prepare for further operations.

On the ground they continued their attacks on the enemy on the eastern and western fronts with the central forces holding their positions on the southern flank. They were taking casualties but enemy casualties were much heavier. A few hours later aircraft were heard overhead then the sounds of the bombs could be heard exploding all along the west, front and eastern sectors. Approximately one hour later the bombing could be heard on the Canadian border. The orders of the field command had been followed. If there was any question about the will of the American army that question had been answered.

On the battlefields the enemy attacks had slowed, at least temporarily, due to the bombing of their positions and the explosions of the cluster bombs and the ten thousand pound bomb to their north.

Commands were given to field commanders on the east and west to launch full attacks on the enemy forces for four hours then hold their positions. This, it was hoped, would further slow enemy attacks from those positions. No one really expected their actions could prevent the eventual loss to the enemy but all were determined to make them pay as heavy a price as possible.

Independent central command ordered all remaining bomber aircraft at the Ohio air base, still capable of flight, to reload and stand ready. Personnel at the Ohio air base were advised to monitor air traffic from Canada and be prepared to intercept any that entered American air space in support of enemy forces. One unarmed reconnaissance plane was ordered to make a daily flight over the Canadian border to monitor the positions of enemy forces in Canada. The Canadian media was telling the world leaders about the bombing attack carried out by the American barbarians. Claiming tens of thousands of innocent civilians and military personnel were murdered by the bombings.

For decades Moslem immigrants from the Arabic states had poured into Canada and now were the majority in that country. Their parliament, now controlled by Moslem citizens, issued a call for Moslems from all over the world to come to Canada and support the United Nations in their efforts to rid the world of the American Christian tyrants. And so they came, by boats and by air. Tens of millions of Moslem immigrants from eastern European states, Asia and the mid east states poured into Canada. Bringing their anti God, anti Christian and anti American hatred with them.

Independent reconnaissance flights reported United Nations armies had entered Wisconsin and were moving towards Ohio. They also revealed the United Nations armies had came across the border and were now moving thru western New York into Pennsylvania heading for Ohio. It was now only a matter of days until these overwhelming numbers would reach the battlefields in Ohio.

All aircraft at the Ohio base were ordered to commence round the clock bombing runs at the enemy forces. Long range bombers were ordered to attack the United Nations armies moving out of Wisconsin, Illinois and Pennsylvania to slow their advance.

The short range fighters and bombers were ordered to attack local enemy forces as close to friendly lines as possible without let up. Once all aircraft had completed their missions and exhausted their fuel, munitions and supplies they were told to abandon the base and rejoin their families.

Field commanders were advised of conditions they would soon be facing. They were advised that they would soon be facing overwhelming numbers and face certain annihilation. It was agreed that once the bombing of enemy positions commenced all commanders would order their men to abandon their positions, retreat and disperse and try to make their way back to their homes and families. It was their hope that the heavy bombing would keep the enemy they were facing occupied giving their men time to evacuate and escape.

The end was approaching for these honorable men who had fought a valiant fight against overwhelming odds. They had lost more than half their number in the years of fighting. It was for most a sad day to admit they no longer had the capacity to continue the struggle. But all agreed, the time had come to return to their homes to prepare for life under the rule of a United Nations world order whose leaders were a mixture of Communist, Socialists and Moslem.

When the sounds of approaching aircraft and exploding bombs commenced the orders were given to abandon their positions. Throughout the day and night the pilots did their jobs keeping up a constant attack upon the enemy forces. The independent forces withdrew and dispersed, scattering through the southern Ohio and Kentucky fields and communities. Their homes and families were as far away as Texas in the west to Maine in the northeast. None knew what awaited them. Whether their homes and families would still be there, or how they would survive in a country that had been destroyed by the socialists thirst for power.

The years of war had left America in ruins. The states declaring their independence had waged a desperate fight for liberty but uncertain times now lay ahead for all of what was America. History would certainly record, that the reluctance of the people to oppose enslavement at the beginning, led to the defeat and collapse of America. Had the people stood as one against the rise of socialism in Washington the years of fighting and loss of life would not have occurred.When the bombing had ended United Nations armies were joined by the military forces coming out of Canada. But the enemy was no more. The fighting was over. When advised that all hostilities had ended United Nations leaders in Canada and around the world began their preparations for domination of America, and the world. With America destroyed no other nation dared defy the leaders of the new world order.

They ordered their armies to divide and relocate in the capital cities of each state to restore order to the land. Another five million civilian and military advisors were brought to the former nation of America and joined their armies in the cities and states across the land of what was once America. The former Washington socialists were ordered moved from Florida and relocated in the Washington capital buildings. Within weeks United Nations leaders moved from Canada to Washington to meet with the former rulers of America.

The leaders of the United Nations, wanting complete loyalty from the citizens of this land, issued the call for one hundred fifty million immigrants from socialist and Moslem states around the world, to come to this new land. The radical socialists now in control welcomed this destruction of the old America. Tens of millions began the move entering thru the eastern and western seaports of what was once America. Over a span of months the total population doubled to more than six hundred million, with more than two hundred million of Moslem beliefs clearly now the majority.

Those of the Christian faith of European ancestry were now a minority. African Americans citizens soon began mass conversions into the Moslem beliefs. Many others left to return to the land of their ancestors. With the destruction of America the economies of nations the world over were in ruins. Under the control of United Nations appointees the rebuilding began. Agricultural lands now were turned into state controlled communal farms where former farmers worked alongside immigrants under the control of appointed managers.

Small shops reopened with many now operated by foreign immigrants. Industries began rebuilding under the supervision of mostly Asian managers. A peace was restored to the land as the people slaved and starved in fear of government.

As the former independent fighters found their way home many found their towns now occupied by strangers from foreign lands. Many of their families had died from the starvation, disease and pestilence.

After weeks of discussions it was decided the president would remain in office as prime minister, however, would serve at the convenience of the UN General Assembly. The congress would remain as a body renamed the national parliament. Changes were made to reduce the number of members to one representative from each state. Parliamentary members would serve at the convenience of the UN General Assembly. Their immediate priorities would be to insure the constitution and all existing federal and state laws were abolished, and replaced with the international civil and criminal laws established by the United Nations charter.

It was decided each state would have a governor, appointed by the prime minister, and approved by the general assembly. All state, county, and local law enforcement personnel would take their orders from, and serve at the pleasure of the governor. Their primary duties would be to enforce the international laws within their states and maintain order within their districts. A United Nations appointee would command all state national guard units. Comprised of former United Nations military forces.

These units would be subordinate to the governors for his use in quelling insurrection attempts and suppress violence wherever necessary.

The United Nations Security Council announced that those appointed to positions of authority within the central and state governing bodies, including the enforcement bodies comprised of UN soldiers, would remain for an indefinite period. Once conditions warrant, national elections would be held to permit the people to elect their own national governing body, to include a prime minister and general assembly. Those elected bodies would then have the authority to appoint state governors and form state enforcement bodies to replace those currently serving.

After elections are held, those elected to serve as prime minister and in the general assembly would be responsible for insuring all international treaties adopted by the United Nations were complied with and Insuring that all international criminal and civil laws were enforced.

They would at all times be responsible for furnishing military and financial support to the world governing body, military forces and equipment so furnished would be under the control of the United Nations commanders.

The taxing authority of the United Nations had been adopted at an earlier convention. That treaty authorized the general assembly to impose an international tax upon all member states of the United Nations. And to impose trade sanctions on any non member states. Taxes were levied on all international exports and imports of goods and services and each member state was taxed according to the state of their economies and financial resources.

The United Nations General Assembly approved the implementation of the tax immediately. The taxing authority was instituted and became the law of the world.

Now the people were being openly taxed to support the new world order. Like their ancestors whose taxes were taken to England to support the king, American taxes were now going to support the New World Order. The American people were now outnumbered and enslaved under a New World Order, Controlled by Moslem Socialists and former Communist who hated America.

Then the cleansing began. The American people had long past surrendered their firearms. Helpless in the face of overwhelming hordes of armed Moslems they suffered the fate that other Christians existing within the confines of a Moslem controlled state. Millions were exterminated by the Moslem extremists, those who escaped death were sentenced to submit to enslavement.

The influx of immigrants from United Nations sponsoring states guaranteed the election of leaders loyal to the cause of world socialism. One year later national elections were held to elect a prime minister and members of the parliament. Americas governmental leaders found themselves replaced by those elections, with long time United Nations Moslem underlings, who's loyalties to the United Nations general assembly were well known. Military forces, mostly of Moslem ancestry, dressed in the United Nations green uniforms, and commanded by United Nations command personnel patrolled the towns and cities of what was once America. All government enforcement agencies and communications media were now controlled by United Nations appointed command personnel.

The goals of worldwide socialism as dreamed of by Karl Marx, and pursued by members of the Council on Foreign Relations had been accomplished. The indoctrination of American youth into the world of anti Christian paganism had worked. The America of our fathers had collapsed. Destroyed from within by the malaise of an apathetic people.

With America destroyed, the last defender of Christianity was gone. The people of the state of Israel, surrounded on all sides by enemies, with no one left to protect them, turned their eyes to the skies. But alas, there shall be three and one half years of false peace for them, followed by three and one half years of promised tribulations, before the Savior shall appear.

One final word of caution. If you believe what I have written, that America will be overcome by United Nations sponsored Islamic Socialists, could never happen consider this. The population of England, France, and Germany are now threatened by a near majority of their populations being of Moslem ancestry. The Moslem immigration into Australia now threatens the democratic form of government in that country. Even more dangerous to the future of America, the total Islamic Moslem population in Canada now exceeds, by some reports, the population of Canadians of European ancestry.

With a Moslem majority on our border in Canada, and no immigration policy existing or enforced in America, freedom will not last for a disarmed America.

Authors Viewpoint

In conclusion I can only offer these words of advice to the reader, and the American people. It was our forefathers faith and strength that led and won the fight for independence. It was their courage and wisdom that led to the ratification of our constitution. They were the founders of our country and our system of government. They were men of great courage, principle and wisdom. I advise you to read their words and hold them forever in your hearts.

Listen as they speak: We the people, of the United States, in order to form a more perfect union, establish justice, insure domestic tranquility, provide for the common defense, promote the general welfare, and secure the blessings of liberty to ourselves and posterity, do ordain and establish this constitution for the United States of America. That Constitution was then ratified on the fourth day of March in the year of our Lord, 1789. Who were these men who fought for their independence and gave us our free country, with a constitution to keep us free?

America was founded by Christian men with Christian principles. The Constitution they gave us bears witness to their intent. Consider these words taken from the declaration of independence. We hold these truths to be self evident, that all men are created equal, that they are endowed by their creator, with certain unalienable rights, that among these are Life, Liberty and the Pursuit of happiness. Remember, your rights are endowed by your creator, not by Washington or the United Nations, as some would have it be.

Remember these words from the declaration of independence. They clearly show their intent to vest the power of government into the hands of the people: They wrote, "that to secure these rights, Governments are instituted among men, deriving their just powers from the consent of the governed". Remember and hear these words, they govern by our consent.

Remember also these words from the declaration of independence, "Whenever any Form of Government becomes destructive of these Ends, it is the right of the people to alter or abolish it". I submit, were you to declare your loyalty to their words today, Washington would declare you to be a radical, just as the king of England declared the founders of our nation to be.

Consider the words of section 4, of Article iv of our constitution. "The United States shall guarantee to every state in this union a republican form of government, and shall protect each of them against invasion, and on application of the legislature, or of the executive (when the legislature cannot be convened) against domestic violence". America has been invaded by fifty million criminals pouring across our southern borders. All with the full knowledge and consent of the seated congresses and several presidents during the past three decades.

I would remind you that Article six of Our constitution requires that" The Senators and Representatives, and all executives (including the president) and judicial officers", shall be bound by oath to support this constitution. I ask you, In view of the aforementioned welcomed, aided and abetted invasion of criminals spreading across our land, would you agree they have failed, and refused, to uphold their oath to protect the constitution and America from that invasion?

Consider this, When a soldier fails to uphold his oath of enlistment on the battlefield, no matter how fearful the conditions, they are charged with desertion and court-martialed. So I ask you, should not the elect be charged and tried for their failure and refusal to uphold their oath of office?

Amendment four (iv) of our constitution states" The right of the people to be secure in their persons, houses, papers, and effects, against unreasonable searches and seizures, shall not be violated, and no warrant shall issue, but upon probable cause, supported by oath or affirmation, and particularly describing the place to be searched, and the persons or things to be seized.

Would you agree that such policies and practices as (random) roadblocks where searches for drivers licenses, proof of insurance and tests for incriminating evidence of Alcohol usage violate the conditions of article four? I can find no words in the constitution that grants government the authority to violate the rights to privacy of all, in the hopes of finding one who has violated some law or government policy.

Lest We forget; Amendment 1, of our constitutional Bill of Rights says; Congress shall make no law respecting an establishment of religion, or prohibiting the free exercise thereof. This should be pretty clear to any rational, reasonable freedom loving person. Congress shall not establish a state religion, and require all citizens to swear allegiance to that religion.

It very clearly says Congress shall not prohibit the free exercise of religion, and that includes our Christian religion.

Yet there are those liberals and socialist in Congress, and their judicial appointees, and the atheistic members of the American Civil Liberties Union, who systematically prohibit the free expression of the Christian faith. And Our government is a member of the United Nations World Order whose charter states, it shall be a crime under international law for parents to compel their children to attend religious services. So I ask you, Are your legislators defending your constitutional right to believe as a Christian? Need I ask, have you been betrayed?

Amendment two (2) of our constitution states," A well regulated militia, being necessary to the security of a free state, the right of the people to keep and bear arms shall not be infringed. Socialists in Washington and in the states have long sought to deny citizens this right claiming this amendment only pertains to the right of the state to form militias. I strongly disagree with their prejudiced interpretation of the Second Amendment, but if we suppose their argument had some merit then I would remind the congress, and you the people, of two other constitutional provisions that protect the people right to keep and bear firearms, and protect that right from infringement.

Amendment 1X of the citizens Bill of Rights included in the constitution states, " The enumeration in the constitution of certain rights, shall not be construed to deny or disparage others retained by the people". In plain language this says, just because certain rights were written into the constitution, does not limit the peoples rights to those enumerated. It does not give government the power to decide, that if a right is not written in the constitution, the people do not have those rights.

Amendment X of the citizens Bill Of Rights, included in the constitution states," The powers not delegated to the Federal Government by the constitution, nor prohibited by it to the states, are reserved to the states or the people". In plain language this statement means, The Federal government has only those powers delegated to it in the constitution. All other powers and rights belong to the states or the people.

In view of the words contained in Bill of Rights Amendments 1X and X to our constitution, do you believe the Federal and State governments have unconstitutionally infringed upon the rights of the people by requiring registration and licensing to have the right to keep and carry a firearm? Lets see what our founding fathers said about this amendment. Listen as they speak: Thomas Jefferson, of Virginia said; No free man shall ever be debarred the use of arms. He also said; Laws that forbid the carrying of arms, disarm only those who are neither inclined nor determined to commit crimes. Such laws make things worse for the assaulted and better for the assailants. They serve, rather than prevent homicides, for an unarmed man may be attacked with greater confidence than an armed man. Jefferson's commonplace book" 1774-1776"

Samuel Adams, of Massachusetts, wrote " The said constitution shall never be construed to infringe the just liberty of the press, or the rights of conscience, or to prevent the people of the United States, who are peaceful citizens, from keeping their own guns. Massachusetts' US Constitutional convention, 1778.

George Mason, of Virginia wrote, "When the resolution of enslaving America was formed in Great Britain, The British parliament was advised by an artful man, who was governor of The commonwealth of Pennsylvania; that forbidding the citizens to have guns was the best and most effectual way to enslave them; but they should not do it openly, but weaken them, and let them sink gradually. I ask, George Mason said, who are the militia, They consist of the whole people. Virginia' US constitution ratification convention, 1778.

Richard Henry Lee, of Virginia wrote; A militia when properly formed are in fact the people themselves, and include all men capable of bearing arms, To preserve liberty it is essential that the whole body of people always posses arms. He added, the mind that aims at a select militia, must be influenced by a truly anti-republican principle. (in other words, those who would limit the ownership and bearing of weapons to a select few controlled by government must be anti-republican). From the Federal Farmer Paper, 1778.

James Madison, of Virginia wrote; The Constitution preserves " the advantage of being armed. Which Americans possess over the people of almost every other nation, where the governments are afraid to trust the people". The Federalist Paper, N0.46.

Trent Coxe, of Pennsylvania wrote, The militia who are in fact the effective part of the people at large, will render many troops quiet unnecessary. They will form a powerful check upon the regular troops, and will generally be sufficient to over-awe them. An American Citizen paper, Oct 21, 1787. (In other words, if sufficient numbers of citizens are armed they will be adequate to keep the government troops in check) and prevent a central government from restricting our liberties.

Fisher Ames, of Massachusetts wrote, "The rights of conscience, of bearing arms, of changing the government, are declared to be inherent in the people". Letter to F. R. Minoe, June 12, 1789.

Patrick Henry, of Virginia wrote; "Guard with jealous attention the public liberty. Suspect everyone who approaches that jewel". Virginia's U. S. Constitution ratification convention records

I could provide the reader with writings from more than two dozen delegates to the constitutional convention, all attesting to their strong beliefs and intentions to protect the rights of the people. Defending your right to keep and bear arms is a right they all agreed upon. All of their writings can be found in the national archives, these statements and writings were made by our fathers and founders to confirm their strong beliefs that only by arming all the people can a people remain free of government oppression.

Their firm belief was that only an armed people can preserve our rights as citizens to insure government governs by the consent of the people. I again remind the reader and the people, read our constitution and Bill of Rights, hold them close to your hearts and minds that no government can ever take your rights from you.

I have spent considerable time discussing the peoples loss of their rights to keep and bear firearms. I felt I must do so because history teaches that an unarmed people are or shall become an enslaved people.

Now Consider this: In the year 2001, the United Nations general assembly adopted a program of actions that promote internal gun control of all legal firearms. It will require national registries for tracking all firearms. It will call for the establishment of an international tracking certificate, monitored by the United Nations, as part of registration. And it will require a comprehensive program of worldwide gun controls, including a ban on private ownership of all guns.

I have no doubt that Washington will eventually sign on with the United Nations gun control policies. And remember, Washington honors their membership in the United Nations.

History has shown that registration is the forerunner, pre-curser, of confiscation. The United Nations, and their Socialists counterparts here in America, are determined to disarm the people of America. They know forty million armed and determined people cannot be overcome and enslaved. Registration is the first step towards reaching their goal of disarming America.

Therefore I call upon every American citizen who loves the rights and liberties we inherited from our forefathers to obtain a copy of the United States Constitution, and our Citizens Bill of Rights Amendments. Study them, keep them secure and be prepared to defend them.

I call upon every American citizen to obtain a copy of the United Nations Charter. I call upon you to obtain a copy of every one of the more than five hundred multi national treaties Washington has agreed to, some in secrecy without public hearings or discussions. I urge you to read and study these agreements and compare them to our Constitution. I believe when you do, you will agree we have been betrayed by the Washington Socialists .

I call upon you, every citizen who enjoys and wants their children to enjoy, the freedoms and liberties endowed by our creator, to contact every legislator between your home and Washington. Demand that we withdraw our membership in the United Nations. Demand that we revoke every UN treaty or policy Washington has agreed to. Demand that our constitution and our national sovereignty be returned to the people, and safeguarded for our children.

I believe it is crucial to the survival of America for every honest adult citizen to purchase a hunting rifle. I urge you, do so now while it is still legal to purchase a firearm. Do so now while firearms are still available in America. Practice with them and keep them in a secure place.

I urge you to refuse to register them when the Socialist order you to do so. I urge you to refuse to surrender them when the socialist come for them. In the words of Patrick Henry, I urge you to guard with jealous attention any who approach that public jewel. Be prepared to defend your rights, your freedoms, your liberties and our constitution when the only thing that stands between liberty and enslavement is an armed people.

A free America is our birthright, it was given to us by our Lord, and preserved for us by the strength and courage of our forefathers. We must have the courage and faith to honor our founders and preserve a free America for our children.

And now, May our God who created all things in Heaven and Earth, strengthen you and keep you in the days of trials to come.

THE END

www.ingramcontent.com/pod-product-compliance
Lightning Source LLC
Chambersburg PA
CBHW061314280526
45784CB00002B/981